TRACK AND FIELD
For Girls and Women

by

NELL C. JACKSON, Ph.D.

Department of Physical Education
University of Illinois
Urbana, Illinois

Burgess Publishing Company

426 South Sixth Street • Minneapolis, Minn. 55415

Physical Education Consultant to the Publisher:

ELOISE M. JAEGER, Ph. D.
Department of Physical Education for Women
University of Minnesota

Library of Congress Catalog Card Number 68-15813

FOREWORD

The elements of running, jumping, and throwing inherent in track and field events make these activities the most ancient practiced and played by man. The struggle against the environment — ferocious battle against animals needed for food and rivalry against other humans for survival — have been replaced in the modern setting by competition against artificial environmental hazards of obstacles and objects, fervent battle against one's own previous time and space performance "records," and rivalry against other humans for the "prize" of winning.

The recent phenomenal upsurge of interest and activity in girls' and women's track and field events may be traced to several factors. One is the attention drawn by the poor showing of the United States Women's Olympic Track and Field Team in comparison to that of the U.S.S.R. women. The resolution to improve our record has accelerated track and field programs throughout our country. A second influence is the recognition of the latent values for fitness of running, jumping, and throwing — common activities in a track and field program. Growing is the understanding that vigorous sports activities are not harmful, but indeed helpful, to maintenance of good health. A third reason is that latitude allowed a sports-minded female in our culture is increasing. The excellence of skilled women performers is becoming more appreciated and admired by both sexes. It is no longer considered unfeminine to compete in highly active and competitive sports. A fourth factor is the enthusiastic promotional efforts by federal, state, and local representatives of associations, agencies, and clubs. Such groups include the American Association for Health, Physical Education and Recreation's Division for Girls' and Women's Sports; the Women's Board of the U.S. Olympic Development Committee; and the Amateur Athletic Union.

The author, Dr. Nell Jackson, has found in track and field a dominant life interest. She has personally and professionally experienced the nuances of track and field as an Olympic participant, coach, author, lecturer, and workshop consultant. Since winning her first competitive running event at the age of fourteen, she has gone on to become a representative for The United States on the 1948 Women's Olympic Track and Field Team, competing in London, England. The U.S. Women's Olympic Track Team was coached by Miss Jackson in 1956. She also coached the U.S. Olympic Track and Field Team which toured Europe in 1965.

Her teaching and coaching have brought national and international recognition as an expert in track and field. She has authored several articles in major publications and has been a contributing author to track and field in a workbook. Currently she is completing a promotional film, *Grace in Motion,* for the United States Olympic Development Committee. As chairman of the Liaison Area for Division of Girls' and Women's Sports of the American Association for Health, Physical Education and Recreation, she has worked with many official organizations mutually interested in furthering sports for girls and women. She is currently a member of the U.S. Olympic Games Planning Committee, U.S. Women's Olympic Track and Field Committee, Women's Board of the U.S. Olympic Development Committee and is serving as Chairman for the AAU Women's Track and Field Committee.

As well as a frequent workshop consultant in track and field, she has served in that capacity in the First National Institute in 1963 and has spoken at the Second, Third, and Fourth National Institute during the ensuing years.

Dr. Jackson's strength in theory and practice of track and field has been enhanced through graduate preparation in biomechanics, physiology, and prescribed exercise first at Springfield College where she received her Master of Science degree in Physical Education and later at the State University of Iowa where she earned her Doctor of Philosophy degree in Physical Education.

There is, perhaps, no one in the area of women's track and field more qualified to write this kind of greatly needed text than Dr. Jackson. This work, devoted to helping the teacher, coach, and performer achieve a greater depth of understanding, is a landmark in the field.

Dr. Alyce Cheska, Head
Department of Physical Education for Women
University of Illinois, Urbana, Champaign

PREFACE

This book is written with the idea of helping the physical education teacher and the young athlete understand the mechanics of track and field. As they begin to grasp the principles, a clearer insight will be obtained and they will be able to apply these principles as they teach and perform each skill.

The major areas of running, jumping, and throwing are analyzed by illustrating and explaining the mechanical principles involved in the various movements. This is followed by a logical sequence of progressions which may be used as a guide in teaching the individual skills in a class situation as well as in a competitive situation.

In using this book it is not suggested that you transcribe the mechanical principles to your students and athletes as they are presented; rather, by understanding the simple mechanics involved in the various movements, you will be able to communicate to them in descriptive terms that they will be able to understand. At the same time, it will stimulate them to the point of eliciting a positive response.

In order to perform successfully in the events found in the track and field program, the teacher must understand the importance of the proper sequence and timing of all movements. Therefore, they must be able to breakdown the whole movement into a series of smaller units then build them up again. If this is not done, often the entire sequence is lost and timing is destroyed. When teaching track and field one often finds that it is an endless pattern of whole-part-whole learning with each new whole and each new part more meaningful than those parts which preceded it.

In a teaching situation, one of the advantages of track and field is that it can serve a large number of people of varying abilities. Each person should participate in the program because of a desire to enjoy the movements found within it. One should always be encouraged to participate within the realm of her ability. Her success is measured by this ability, not necessarily by the performance against a highly skilled person. If a girl learns to high jump three feet, then this is success for her and it means just as much as the five foot jump performance by another girl.

The author wishes to express her appreciation to the students and colleagues who in direct and indirect ways have contributed to this book. Grateful acknowledgement is also extended to Mr. Michael Alisandrelli who completed the illustrations and Mr. Eli Attar for the photographs taken during competition.

The author also wishes to thank the Women's Board of the U.S. Olympic Development Committee for permission to reprint the Conditioning and Training chapter which appears in the Proceedings of the Second National Institute on Girls' Sports.

TABLE OF CONTENTS

LIST OF TABLES

LIST OF FIGURES

TRACK AND FIELD

For Girls and Women

Chapter 1

CONDITIONING
AND TRAINING

O. William Dayton, Head Athletic Trainer at Yale University, has summarized the effects of training and conditioning in one statement: "There are as many conditioning programs as there are coaches and trainers. We know that sports basically require physical strength, endurance, and skills. The better the condition of the athlete, the longer he participates; the poorer the condition of the athlete, the quicker he retires. The individuals who are in good physical condition are the athletes who compose our teams today: the group lacking this physical conditioning falls by the wayside and they do not participate in athletics very long." (8)

Conditioning may be defined as preparing the body for activity, such as improving one's strength, endurance, flexibility, and speed. Training, on the other hand, may be defined as the process of adjusting to the competitive situation and improving in the skills in which the athlete is to perform. (2)

Even though by definition the terms, conditioning and training, appear to be different, they are often used synonymously. For some people, they are usually considered as being so closely allied in preparing an athlete for competition that no distinction is made between them. For example, as an athlete undergoes certain forms of physical movements in acquiring a skill, she also improves the quality of her muscles while using the same movements. Thus, while training she is also improving her condition.

From the coach's point of view, when preparing an athlete for competition, the problem of conditioning and training presents a logical sequence. The body, as a machine, must be strong enough to overcome the processes of fatigue to such an extent that the performance of the skills will not be hampered by the lack of these qualities. Theoretically, a person can be in excellent condition and still not be trained in any skill, *and*, on the other hand, she may be well trained to perform a specific skill *but* lack the physical capacity necessary to complete the performance or to continue the performance for any length of time. A girl may come out to track practice everyday and receive the best education in track techniques that the coach is capable of giving. As a result of this she is capable of demonstrating a very highly skilled performance. Her mechanics of movement are refined to the utmost degree. However, if upon leaving the track, she continually violates good hygienic habits, she will reduce her condition. She may look like another Wilma Rudolph for the first 25 yards of a race, but she will find it difficult to maintain that pace over a longer distance without adequate conditioning; she will lose ground and come in last. True, conditioning requires months to achieve, but it can be destroyed within a few days. We know that a sprinter reaches her maximum acceleration point about 50-60 yards from the start of a race, therefore, the winner of the race will be the one who can maintain this speed (maximum acceleration) over the longest distance or throughout the latter part of the race.

Some conditioning techniques may be used as general training techniques and some of the training techniques may be used for conditioning. Because of this possibility, the terms are used synonymously from a general point of view; the teacher and coach will be free to adapt the techniques to their immediate situation — for conditioning or training. When considering the finer points of training, the teacher will have to deal with each event separately because it is foolish to think that one can train a sprinter in the same manner as a high jumper or discus thrower.

For many years, teachers and coaches have been constantly searching for one conditioning and training procedure that would produce maximum efficiency in the shortest possible time. They have been putting popular training theories to the "test of experience." Many people would agree with Roger Bannister that "training methods — are likely to remain empirical — because they are dependent upon more factors than it is possible to analyze at present."(11) However, we must realize that there have been noticeable advancements in the efficiency of conditioning and training through the application of scientific data along with the accumulation of experience and tradition.

The perfect training system will never be found, for there are several methods that will give the same results. However it has been observed that some individuals adjust to one method much better than others.

In recent years, the tendency has been to place more demands upon the athlete in regard to the performance of work. Not too many years ago, an athlete's fitness was thought to depend to a large extent upon regulation of his food, drink, and sleep. Undue physical activity was looked upon as a possible cause of energy drainage. Now, it is recognized that only through work, assuming that one has adequate rest and nutrition, can the powers of the muscular and circulatory systems develop to their highest capacities. Look at the records that have been broken over the years. Top U.S. girls (runners) are faster today than the top men (runners) were at the turn of the century.

Today, the teachers and coaches are indebted to the area of sports medicine because it has given the group a definite concept of the enormous adaptive possibilities of the body as a result of training.

Many physiological responses are altered by training and conditioning. Lucien Brougha (10) has indicated that as a result of training, the improvement in each bodily system is about 25 per cent or less; however, when combined, all of the effects may result in an improvement of the total performance which may be as high as 100 per cent.

The principal qualities of the adaptation of the body through training that are known at present are: (10)

1. An increase in the strength of the muscles and improved neuromuscular coordination.
2. A greater mechanical efficiency as measured in terms of lower oxygen consumption for a given amount of work. (With this there is improvement of the precision and the economy of any motion or sequence of motions involved in muscular activity.)
3. A greater maximum oxygen consumption.
4. A higher maximum cardiac output with less increase in pulse rate and blood pressure during submaximal exercise.
    (The heart becomes more efficient and is able to circulate more blood while beating less frequently.)
    Incidentally, this greater efficiency of the heart enables a larger blood flow to reach the muscles, ensuring an increased supply of fuel and oxygen and permitting the individual to reach a higher level of performance.
5. Improved pulmonary ventilation permitting adequate oxygen and carbon dioxide exchange for lower energy expenditures of the respiratory pump.
6. Quicker recovery in pulse rate and blood pressure after submaximal exercise (a faster recovery after exertion.)
    Considering these physiological effects of training, it is essential that the performer be 100 percent fit when preparing for an athletic event.

An analysis of the factors which contribute to success in athletic performances has shown that strength is extremely important. This is not surprising, however, when you consider the structure of the body. The bones are attached in such a way that they form levers which are moved by the muscles. The levers employed in sports, such as those of arms and legs, are of the type in which the muscle is attached near the end of the bone. The weight to be lifted is at the free end of the lever far away from the muscle which is to move the weight. (8)

Conditioning exercises should be easy to perform, and they should utilize the large muscles since it is through the activity of these muscles that general physical condition is most improved.

General fitness is the foundation on which the structure of technical skills can be built. You can not cut corners or take too many short cuts. If that foundation is insecure, the entire building will collapse. This is what happens to the body. An athlete who is not completely fit will never develop the potential of which she is capable and, in addition to other things, she will be more liable to injury.

Forbes Carlile (5) has listed some principles of training. These principles should be employed in the best training methods:

1. The training load must be severe and must be applied frequently enough and with sufficient intensity to cause the body to adapt maximally to a particular activity.

2. Individuals react differently to the same training load. The most important consideration must be how the individual is responding to training without strain or whether the body is slowly losing its capacity to adjust itself. Therefore, TRAINING WILL ALWAYS BE AN INDIVIDUAL PROBLEM. Training must be tailored to suit the individual for best results.

    There are many factors which should be taken into account in drawing up a detailed schedule. Some of these factors include age of the athlete, time spent at everyday work and studies, athlete's physical make-up, time available for sleep and rest, and training facilities available.

3. Exercises involved in training are only one of a number of stresses acting on the athlete. All stresses must be considered when appraising the effect on training. For example, the wear and tear stress of daily traveling and manual labor must be overcome by the body.

    Psychological factors are very important in training also because emotional conditions affect bodily functions and can be powerful stressing agents.

4. Too much stress on the individual causes strain, and strain lowers the performance level. The signs and symptoms of strain are many and varied. Some can be felt and thus appreciated by the performer. Others can be measured.

5. Recuperation periods are essential both during a single training session and throughout the year. Rest, with consequent physical and mental relaxation, must be carefully blended with doses of exercise. A rhythmical cycle of exercise and recuperation should be established both within individual training periods and week by week.

6. Training is specific. Although there is a certain amount of carry-over, as a rule the best training for a particular sport is not of much use for another. Swimming training will not help the high jumper — nor fencing help the basketball player. Carrying this concept further, we find that within a particular sport, training is specific. For instance, sprinters do not follow the same training pattern as middle distance runners. Every event requires special preparation.

7. Strengthening and flexibility exercises are very beneficial. These two types of training carried out mainly in the off-season should be carefully designed and directed at specific groups of muscles and joints.

    Looseness and a high degree of flexibility mean free-flowing movements. It is now clearly established that great strength, brought about by resistance exercises (e.g. weight training), improves performance in many fields. Scientifically designed weight training with appropriate stretching exercises, will not slow down the sportsman or cause "muscle-bound" condition, nor will they cause bulging muscles on girls. Girls working on a progressive resistance exercise program could increase their strength 43 per cent over a five week period without any notice-able changes in the size of their muscles. (9)

8. INTERVAL training is one of the most important individual items in the modern training schedule. This consists funda-mentally of rhythmically carrying out an activity from 30 seconds to one minute at fairly intense effort (but not all-out). Each exercise period is followed by 10 seconds to two minutes of slow recuperative activity.

9. Nutrition plays a major role in physical performance. The first requirement in diet is a variety of foods with as many as possible in their natural state.

    Today, there are THREE popular conditioning and training techniques. They are listed as (1) circuit training, (2) interval training, and (3) fartlek.

    All of these techniques are flexible enough to fit into the ca-tegory of conditioning or training . . . even though the first two have the term training in their title. If these techniques are applied correctly, they will improve strength, flexibility, and endurance.

CIRCUIT TRAINING

Circuit training is probably one of the newest training methods and it has a wide appeal. The appeal is so wide that it is being applied in principle to all forms of athletic activities. It is a form of general fitness training based on sound physiological principles; it offers the kind of varied activities and continuous challenges that are attractive to large numbers of young people, many of whom show little enthusiasm for ordinary forms of physical training. (11)

A. It develops muscular and circulatory-respiratory fitness.
B. It applies the principle of progressive loading a muscle.
C. It enables large numbers of performers to train at the same time by employing a circuit of consecutively numbered exercises around which each performer progresses, doing a prescribed allocation of work at each station and checking the progress against the clock.

The number of exercises in the circuit varies with the amount of time available, the equipment, and the requirements of the performer; however, there are usually ten exercises.

The performer first learns all of the exercises in the circuit, then is tested on each one to obtain the work rate. After this, training on the circuit is encouraged until the performer can complete three laps at the training rate in a specified time, usually 15 minutes, which is known as target time. As the performer becomes stronger, she increases both the number of repetitions and the quality of the exercise. The number of circuits remains at three.

Circuit exercises should be selected and arranged in such a way that they blend into a period of training which will have a positive effect upon all-round strength, muscular endurance, general cardiovascular endurance, and power.

Some controversial exercises are often included in the circuit; be aware of them and treat them accordingly. The deep knee bend and duck walk which have been used traditionally as training activities for sports are now generally disapproved by medical authorities. Both exercises have the potential to injure the internal and supporting structures of the knee joint, one of the most vulnerable parts of the athlete's body. (1)

In the deep knee bend, the athlete moves alternately from a standing position to a full squat; in the duck walk, he travels about while trying to maintain the full squat position. Both exercises involve complete flexion and often twisting of the knee which can result in culmulative deterioration or immediate injury to the meniscus (cushioning cartilage) of the joint. The incidence of such meniscal injury following the use of these exercises is sufficient to warrant dropping them from the training program. (1)

In addition to their injury hazard, the deep knee bend and the duck walk have questionable values as conditioning exercises. Few of the sports in which one usually participates involve complete flexion of the knee.

Many other exercises, not carrying the same injury hazard as the duck walk and deep knee bend, are known for athletic conditioning. Information can be found in many of the references on fundamental conditioning exercises and athletic training procedures.

INTERVAL TRAINING

Like all training methods, interval training expanded empirically. The practical interpretation of interval training seems simple. The performer is required to run "at a reasonable" speed over a fixed distance. This run is repeated after a short recovery interval; the number of repetitions are limited. There are four variable situations in interval training: (1) the length of the distance (100 yards, or one or two laps around the gym); (2) the chosen speed (pace – 3/4 of maximum effort); (3) the duration of the recovery interval (one-five minutes); and (4) the number of repetitions (six to ten times).

The athlete is constantly running shorter distances at a faster speed than her competitive pace, and longer distances at a pace slower than her competitive pace.

Interval training may be used by all participants in the track and field program. The procedures of interval training are as varied as the ingenuity of the coaches' minds. One thing to remember is the reason for using this method of training. Here are examples of interval techniques:

1. *Distance* (to build endurance)

    The distance should be long enough to create stress within the runner. Determine the distance to be run, then fix the time. Example: 440 yards in 90 seconds or 220 yards in 40 seconds. Alternate with slow jogging: repeat as many times   as possible, or fix the number of repetitions.

2. *Speed*

    The runner increases her speed over a designated distance that is within her ability to repeat. Example: 220 yards repeated six times at 30 seconds — allowing rest between each run.

3. *Number of Repetitions*
      The number of repetitions depends upon the basic intended value or purpose. There is no magic number or answer. Some coaches will build up the over-all repetitions to equal two and one-half to five times the total competitive distance.

4. *Rest or Recovery Period*
      The recovery interval is gradually reduced as training progresses. Example: 6 x 220 at 30 seconds with decreasing periods of recovery.

Other interesting combinations of techniques include:

1. Use of sets: Two to six runs in each set. 3 x 220 at 30 seconds with three minutes of recovery interval followed by jogging for ten minutes, then the set is repeated again.

2. "Follow the Leader": Have groups of four to five run in a line around the track. The pace of the run is determined by the first runner. The last runner moves up after each lap and becomes the leader (pace setter).

3. Wind-sprints: Repeatedly run sprints (30 - 150 yards) over a short distance until winded (picking up speed along the way).

4. Ins-and-Outs: Alternate fast 100's with slow 100's.

5. Back to Back: Repeatedly run sprints over a short distance; walk back to the start and repeat until winded.

6. Continuous Relay: Assign eight runners to pass the baton together. Each person will run 50 yards then pass off. This is repeated several times before stopping.

7. Medley Relay: Pace work — two teams are paired in terms of ability. Each pair is told to run a designated distance in a given time. Example: First pair will run 110 yards in 13 seconds; second pair — 110 yards in 15 seconds; third pair — 220 yards in 27 seconds; and fourth pair — 440 in 60 seconds.

FARTLEK (Swedish for Speed Play)

Fartlek is free-relaxed running. It is done on a soft surface over an area that permits a great deal of uphill and downhill running. It is a combination of much easy running mixed with fast sprints and periods of resistance running up hills. The advantages of fartlek is that a lot of good solid running can be done without boredom.

The advocates of fartlek indicate that this is the way young children play and develop. There are periods of hard play (running), then periods of rest when they feel tired. It is a continuous cycle of activity.

The running is done on terrain away from the track in a cross country type of environment. Specific intervals are not necessary but the following schedule should be included:

1. Easy running from five to ten minutes;
2. Steady, fast running;
3. Easy running with wind sprints of 50 to 60 yards;
4. Rapid walking for about five minutes;
5. Up-hill running; and
6. A fast pace for about one minute

The general idea is not to exhaust, but rather to stimulate, the runner.

Basic conditioning and training for jumping and throwing events will not vary too much from that for running, that is exercises and forms of running. Jumpers need to build up their legs and should do a great deal of running, including pop-ups (short runs with high jumps). However, special emphasis is given to efficiency of skill and style as well as speed; therefore, they will work on their approach, body position in the air, and landing techniques.

Throwers will have the usual warm-ups, including exercises and jogging, along with some forms of sprinting. Participants in these events spend their time on (1) preliminary throws for form (easy putting); (2) throwing or putting with meet momentum for form (not distance — concentrating again on technique); (3) throwing or putting for form and condition; and (4) working on other events or exercises with a deliberate attempt to build up coordination, speed, and strength.

Training programs for runners, jumpers, and throwers are arranged to run time trials, to jump for height or distance, and to throw for distance a limited number of times during a week — usually once or twice a week.

As mentioned earlier, there are many systems of training. Bill Bowerman of the University of Oregon has developed a method of integrating the various systems into one. (See Table I) This system is a good guide in developing a training schedule. It is best described for training middle distance runners. The goal will change each month. All relative workouts are done at this pace. (See Table I) Within each month, there is a variation in the overall mileage covered. The work schedule for an 880 yard run is written on the form to show how it may be used. A brief interpretation of the schedule is listed below:

1. Distance of the run — 880 yards.
2. Time goal — 2:20 (with relatively even pacing 220 = 35 sec.; 440 = 70 sec.; and 660 = 1:45 sec.).

DATE	DAILY WORK SCHEDULE					GOAL
4/5/	1;3	9B	11C	17	30	2:20

TABLE I

Name _____

1. Warm up
2. Fartlek (light)
3. Jogging and Stretching Exercises
4. High Knee and Fast Leg
5. Wind Sprints
   A. Straight
   B. Curves
6. Sprint Drill: High Knee Lift, Strong Push with Ankle
7. Repeats:

A.	55	C.	150
B.	100	D.	220

8. Repeats: 110

A-20	C-16	E-12
B-18	D-14	

9. Repeats: 220

A.	38	C.	33	E.	29	G.	27
B.	35	D.	31	F.	28	H.	26

10. Repeats: 330

A.	54	C.	50	E.	46	G.	42
B.	52	D.	48	F.	44	H.	40

11. Repeats: 440

A.	75	C.	70	E.	64	G.	60
B.	72	D.	68	F.	62	H.	58

12. Repeats: Selected longer distances
13. Sets:

	660	440	220
A	2:00	80	40
B	1:52	74	36
C	1:50	70	34
D	1:45	68	32
E	1:42	66	30
F	1:36	62	28

14. Bunches:
    2 or 3 660s; 3 to 6 440s; 6 to 10 220s; Use same time as (13) A, B, etc.
15. Reduced intervals: 440s
    Run 440, rest 110, run 440, Use letters as in (11).

DATE	DAILY WORK SCHEDULE					GOAL
4/5/	1;3	9B	11C	17	30	2:20

16. Up and down hill
17. Grass run
18. Relay work:
    A. walk   C.   55
    B. trot   D.   110
19. 3/4 speed over
    A. 220   C.   300
    B. 250   D.   500
20. Test effort:
    A. Full distance at 7/8
    B. First 1/2
    C. Last half
    D. 1st 3rd
    E. Last 3rd
21. Finish work at 70 to 100 percent effort
    50 to 70 yds. at 3/4 effort
    last 50-30 yds. at 9/10 effort
22. Hurdle test effort (50 yds.) (80m)
    A. Full distance all out
    B. First 1/2
    C. First 3rd
23. Work trail-leg over side of hurdle
24. "Five steps" between hurdles
25. Back to back sprinting
    A. 50 yds.
    B. 70 yds.
26. Grass
    A. Similated starts
    B. 60s
27. 3 or 4 hurdles
28. Broad jump technique
    A. Check mark
    B. Take off
    C. Flight
    D. Landing
29. High jump
    A. Approach
    B. Approach with kick-spring
    C. Jump for style at moderate height
    D. Concentrate on take-off leg clearance
    E. Jump under meet conditions
30. Warm down

TABLE II

THE EQUALIZER

A Formula for an Individual Goal

100 yd. Dash

50 yd. world record 5.7	11.4
5.7	-10.3 world record 100 yd.
11.4 sec.	1.1 sec. = 1.0 equalizer

Double the 50 yd. time - 1 sec. = 100 yd. *Goal*
ex: 6.0 x 2 = 12.0 - 1.0 = 11.0
      7.0 x 2 = 14.0 - 1.0 = 13.0

220 yd. Dash

100 yd. world record 10.3	22.9 world record 220 yds.
10.3	-20.6
20.6	2.3 = 2.0 equalizer

Double the 100 yd. time + 2.0 = 220 yd. *Goal*
ex: 11.5 x 2 = 23.0 + 2 = 25.0
      12.0 x 2 = 24.0 + 2 = 26.0

440 yd. Run

220 yd. world record 22.9	52.4 world record 440 yd. run
22.9	-45.8
45.8	6.6 = 7.0 equalizer

Double the 220 time + 7.0 = 440 yd. *Goal*
ex: 26.0 x 2 = 52.0 + 7.0 = 59.0
      27.2 x 2 = 54.4 + 7.0 = 61.4
      30.0 x 2 = 60.0 + 7.0 = 67.0 or 1:07.0

880 yd. Run

World record 440 = 52.4	2:02.0 world record 880 yd. run
52.4	-1:44.8
104.8 or 1:44.8	17.2 = 17.0 sec. equalizer

Double the 440 time + 17 = 880 yd. *Goal*
   60 x 2 = 2:00 + 17 = 2:17
1:05 x 2 = 2:10 + 17 = 2:27
1:10 x 2 = 2:20 + 17 = 2:37

3. 1 = warm up (routine).
4. 3 = jogging and stretching exercises.
5. 9B = 4 x 220-yards at 35 seconds with a three minute rest between each 220.
6. 11C — 4 x 440 at 70 seconds with a five minute rest between each one.
7. 17 — Easy grass work at 1/2 effort.

A very useful guide called "The Equalizer" (Table 2) which was developed by Jack Griffin, a physical education teacher and coach in Frederick, Maryland, is helpful to the teacher in establishing individual goals for the various running events. "The Equalizer" permits each person to work within her own limits instead of being compared constantly with those who are faster or slower. A girl is interested in running the 880 yard but who has never run over 440 yards may have her goal established by doubling her best 440 time and adding the equalizer of 17 seconds. Thus, if her best time in the 440 was 65 seconds, this figure is doubled to equal 2:10.0 plus 17 seconds equals 2:27.0 as her goal for the moment.

"The Equalizer" may also be used as an evaluative tool in the running events.

Specific training and conditioning combinations for each day cannot be given at this time; however, the following suggestions may be used as a guide:

1. Daily practice schedules may be based on one hour of concentrated work, spread over one and one-half hours.
2. Work dosage for middle distance runners should equal two and one-half to five times the actual competitive distance.

A well-defined conditioning and training program supplemented with running will pay rich dividends because the performers will have improved muscle tone and added body strength that will prove invaluable. The emphasis has been on developing strength, endurance, and flexibility. Teachers should not permit the group to concentrate on one area of the body but try to cover all areas — arms, legs, abdomen, and back. At the same time, do not be afraid to overload the work because it is only through work that success can be achieved.

Conditioning and training are not solely a physical problem. The psychological make-up of the individual needs to be taken into consideration. No two individuals will respond identically to the same training program. Each one has psychological needs that are uniquely her own; however, there are common general motives that are shared by all.

Too often teachers or coaches look at the group as just a physical machine. They are not concerned with the group as individuals. Therefore, very little time is devoted to psychological training of the performer. Each person must be relieved of her psychological pressures in order to accomplish the desired goal.

Any sound approach to training for competition regardless of the sport must be planned deliberately and specifically for the mental factors as well as the physical factors.

In closing, Ken Doherty (7) has said, "Man is not an isolated entity in an antagonistic nature. Rather he and Nature are one; he is in Nature and in no sense can he be apart from or other than Nature. His problem then in all his strivings is to lose self-awareness in an isolated sense and to realize his essential oneness within and without. To take a related example, one might view the awesome power of ocean waves as a conflict between wind, water and shore. But a more holistic and scientific attitude would see them as a perfect natural inter-relationship and interaction between these aspects of a single whole."

The most important factor in a program of training is to be able to achieve physical readiness and psychological readiness when necessary.

A sound program of conditioning and training must be individualized and it must follow a sound plan of action.

BIBLIOGRAPHY

1. American Medical Association: *Tips on Athletic Training IV*. AMA, 1962, p. 11.
2. Armbruster, D., R. Allen and B. Harlen, *Swimming and Diving*, St. Louis: C.V. Mosby Company, 1958, p. 209.
3. Bannister, R.G., *The Advancement of Science*, No. 40, March, 1954.
4. Bowman, John, "Training Can Be Overdone", *Track Techniques*, No. 5, September, 1961, p. 147.
5. Carlile, Forbes, "Ten Principles of Training". *Track Techniques*, No. 1., September, 1960, p. 23.
6. Clarke, Henry H. and D.H. Clarke, *Developmental and Adapted Physical Education*. Englewood Cliffs: Prentice Hall, Inc., 1963, p. 188.
7. Doherty, J. Kenneth, "Training the Mind and Body in Track and Field," *Track Techniques*, No. 4, June, 1961, p. 113.
8. Dayton, O. William, *Athletic Training and Conditioning*. New York: The Ronald Press Co., 1960, p. 40.
9. Jackson, Nell C., *Determination of Amount of Strength Gained in the Quadriceps before Hypertrophy Occurs*. Iowa City: State University of Iowa, 1962 (University Microfilms, No. 63-931).

10. Johnson, Warren, *Science and Medicine of Exercise and Sports.* New York: Harper and Brothers, Publishers, 1960, p. 403.
11. Morgan, R.E. and G.T. Adamson, *Circuit Training.* London: G. Bell and Sons, LTD., pp. 19, 31, and 33.
12. Powell, John T., *Track and Field Fundamentals for Teacher and Coach.* Champaign: Stipes Publishing Co., 1962, 1st edition, p. 91.
13. Track Newsletter, Los Altos; Supplementing Track and Field News. Vol. II, No. 11, p. 58.

Chapter 2

WARMING UP

A great deal of controversy has centered around the value of warm-up activities in relationship to one's physical performance. However, empirical evidence by many coaches, athletes, and teachers has justified the continued emphasis placed upon the need for warming up before engaging in physical activity. Herbert deVries (1) has summarized the following justifiable principles for warming up.

1. Whole body warm-ups that raise muscle and blood (rectal) temperatures can significantly improve athletic performance.
2. Whenever possible, a related warm-up (which raises muscle and blood temperatures) is preferable so that a practice effect may be simultaneously achieved.
3. Warming-up is important for preventing muscle soreness and/or injury.
4. Warming-up procedures must be suited to the individual.
5. Warming-up procedures must be suited to the athletic event.
6. A combination of intensity with duration of warm-up must be achieved resulting in temperature increases in the deep tissues without undue fatigue.
7. Warming-up activities are important in activities that directly involve strength and indirectly in events that have a large element of power or acceleration of body weight.
8. Tissue temperature changes brought about by warming-up probably persist for 45 to 80 minutes.

TYPES OF WARM-UPS

In track and field, as in other sports, the warm up should include movements that will employ all of the muscles expected to be used in the various events.

1. *Jogging*

   Jogging is a series of very slow and short running steps. The foot is used in a manner very similar to walking, heel-toe action. The heel-toe action permits the gastrocnemius and soleus muscles to remain relaxed throughout the movement. Another foot position may also be used in jogging. Instead of the heel-toe action, the foot may be used in a relatively flat position, this is, permitting the heel and toe to touch the ground closer together. The arms are carried in a relaxed manner bent at the elbow. Jogging should take place for 10-15 minutes on a relatively soft surface, such as the grassy infield of a track. Warm up shoes or tennis shoes should be worn.

2. *Exercises*

The exercises used during the warm-up should show some degree of continuity and the movements should flow from one part of the body to the next. Generally, flexibility, strength, and endurance (muscle and cardiovascular) type exercises are used; however, each event will have its own exercises, especially in the strengthening area.

Flexibility-Stretching Exercises

These exercises are used to increase the range of movements in and around specific joints of the body. The movements should be steady and graded, building up progressively as the individual moves along. Care should be taken to avoid strong, jerky movements which would force the stretching of a group of muscles.

A sample of the types of exercises used for a general warm up:

1. *Arm flinging overhead*
   S.P.   – Standing, arms extended, hands crossed in front of body.
   Movt.   – Lift arms laterally over head, emphasizing a good stretch in the shoulder girdle, return arms in front of body.

2. *Arm circling*
   S.P.   – Standing, arms extended shoulder level to the side.
   Movt.   – Circle the arms moving forward, upward, backward, and downward. Describe large circles with the arms.

3. *Trunk rotation*
   S.P.   – Standing, feet astride, arms at sides.
   Movt.   – Bend forward from the waist. Keep the knees straight. Reach toward the ground with the hands. Circle the trunk moving upward to the right, backward, to the left, and downward. The arms remain extended throughout the movement.

4. *Full leg swings*
   S.P.   – Standing.
   Movt.   – Swing the leg forward and backward, emphasize the movement extending from the hip. The forward swings are gradually increased until the foot is swinging as

high as the shoulder. Alternate legs after ten swings.

5.   *Hurdle stretch*

    S.P.   — Sitting on the ground in the hurdle position (one leg is extended in front while the other leg is flexed at the knee and abducted to the side getting as much distance between the thighs as possible).

    Movt. — Bounce forward from the hips and touch the extended foot with the opposite hand at the same time the other arm is extended back with the elbow partially flexed. Alternate the legs after ten bounces. The head should continually touch the knee of the extended leg.

6.   *Trunk and hip twist*

    S.P.   — Back lying, arms extended horizontally, palms down.

    Movt. — Lift the right leg up and touch the left hand, return to starting position. Alternate the action of the leg.

7.   *Sit-up*

    S.P.   — Back lying, legs together and extended, hands clasped behind the neck.

    Movt. — Curl trunk forward and touch the elbows to the knees. Return to starting position. Bend the knees then curl forward again with the elbows touching the knees, return to starting position.

8.   *Stretching lower leg*

    S.P.   — Forward stride position, front knee bent, rear leg straight, toes of rear foot on the same line with the forward foot.

    Movt. — Keeping the trunk erect, bounce forward over the front knee, try to keep the heel of the extended leg in contact with the ground. Alternate the legs after ten easy bounces.

9.   *Skipping*

    S.P.   — Standing.

    Movt. — Move from a light jog to easy skipping with high knee lift. Move the arms loosely in opposition to the legs with exaggerated forward-backward swings.

10. *Run in place*

    S.P.   — Standing.

    Movt. — Gradually build up speed from a slow pace to a brisk one. Emphasize a high knee lift and powerful action of the arms.

Terminate the general warm-up with easy jogging.

Additional warm-ups such as strength and endurance types of activities may be used, however, they will vary with the specific event. At any rate, the value of a thorough warm-up cannot be over emphasized for anyone — sprinters, hurdlers, distance runners, throwers, or jumpers.

Warming-down after an event and practice is often overlooked by most novice performers. This technique is used to allow the performer time to taper off the practice and readjust the body heat rate and breath control to normal living. This is particularly true for endurance type events.

BIBLIOGRAPHY

1.   deVries, Herbert, *Physiology of Exercise for Physical Education and Athletics.* Dubuque, Iowa: Wm. C. Brown Company, Publishers. 1966, p. 379.

Chapter 3

BASIC PRINCIPLES OF RUNNING

Running is one of the few natural activities found in our sport programs today. For some, it is a very simple movement to perform, for others, it is extremely difficult to perform. Perhaps one of the big problems is a tendency to copy the style of some outstanding performers rather than adjusting one's individual style to his physical endowment in an effort to develop the most efficient movements. Individual styles do not conform to a standard pattern because differences such as body build, weight, length of limbs, and strength, influence running style.

BASIC PRINCIPLES

1.   For a given force, a short lever will move faster than a longer lever of the same weight.
2.   An off-centered force applied to the body will impart a turning effect to it.
3.   Speed is the product of the rate and length of stride.
4.   To every action there is an equal and opposite reaction.

The use of the arms and legs as well as the position of the head and trunk are affected by the above principles.

The following discussion will help one to understand how these principles influence the body in motion.

ACTION OF THE ARMS

The arms swing in opposition to the legs. They are bent at the elbow with the forearm and upper arm forming almost a right angle. Carrying the arms in this position creates a shorter lever than if the arms were allowed to drop into a slightly extended position. Hence, they are in a better position to move faster, thereby complementing the action of the legs. (See Figure 1)

The arms swing in a forward and backward direction. As they move forward, the hands move toward a line even with the shoulders and as they move backward the hands pass just behind the hips. Often, the arms will swing toward the midline of the body instead of forward and backward from the shoulder. It is permissible for them to swing in this manner as long as they do not cross the midline of the body. Swinging across the midline of the body will encourage

Figure 1. Good action of the arms

Figure 1a. Poor arm action (tendency to swing across the chest)

lateral rotation or twisting of the trunk. This rotation or twisting movement causes an additional amount of energy to be expended by the runner. (See Figure 1a)

The elbows should be relatively close to the sides. Sometimes there is a tendency for them to swing away from the body. This may be corrected by rotating the hands so that the palms turn up.

The hands will follow the action of the arms. They should be relaxed in a semi-closed position — such as, having the thumb and second finger lightly touching each other, while the other fingers are slightly flexed.

Runners will often hold their hands in a very taut manner, extending the fingers or clutching the hands in a tight fist. Both positions will create tension in the body, which should be corrected as soon as it is noticed because the tension will not isolate itself in the hands. Instead, it will gradually move up the arms to the shoulders and down through the trunk. As the tension passes through the body, the arms will become tight and tired; they will move in a jerky manner instead of a smooth flowing manner. Relaxation comes with considerable practice. As the skills of running are practiced, the teacher should be aware of signs of tension. Conscious relaxation in the neck, shoulders, arms and hands during jogging and sprinting will help to reduce the tension.

The various types of runs require slightly different arm action. For example, in sprinting the action is quite vigorous. The arms are used for drive as well as for balance. In the middle distances and distance events, the action is less vigorous and more relaxed.

POSITIONS OF THE TRUNK

An experienced runner, when viewed from the side, gives an illusion of a pronounced forward lean at the end of the driving phase. (As the body passes over the foot it is driven forward by an extension of the leg.) Once the running stride has been obtained, however, the trunk is carried in a relatively upright position. The actual position of the trunk will vary with each runner because of individual differences in body structure. It should be pointed out that sprinters will often have a greater lean of the trunk than middle distance or distance runners. The lean, however, should not be taught. Instead, it should be emphasized that the lean depends upon the speed of the run as well as the amount of resistance encountered by the runner. Sometimes sprinters will assume a forward lean varying up to about 15 degrees from the vertical, while middle distance runners will have a more vertical trunk position. The extreme leans that are occasionally seen in some sprinters are usually taught by a teacher or coach instead of being a natural position of the trunk assumed by the runner. An exaggerated lean will restrict the amount of knee lift in sprinters and it will also contribute to a loss of balance because of an inability of the center of gravity to remain within the continuously changing base of support.

Even though the trunk is carried in a relatively upright position, it is slightly ahead of the driving foot as the leg extends into the driving phase of the run. The purpose of this trunk position is to place the center of gravity just ahead of the driving foot so that the thrusting action of the leg will drive the body forward instead of upward.

ACTION OF THE LEGS

Speed is the product of the length and frequency of stride. These two factors are influenced by the action of the legs.

The action of the legs may be divided into three phases: (1) supportive, (2) drive, and (3) recovery.

1. *Supportive Phase:* When the foot first touches the ground, the body's weight is taken on the ball or forward half of the foot depending upon the speed of the runner. The leg is partially flexed. As the body rotates over the foot there is a momentary let down to the heel. This relatively flat position of the foot is referred to as the supportive phase.

2. *Driving Phase:* As the body passes over the foot it is driven forward by an extension of the leg. This extension is a combination of a thrusting action initiated by a pushing of the ball of the foot against the ground. The action moves through the hip, leg, and foot to the ground. The amount of speed influences the drive of the leg. Sprinters push with the leg until the knee, ankle, and foot are in full extension, but middle distance runners do not use this much extension.

3. *Recovery Phase:* At the completion of the drive, the leg flexes at the hip, knee, and ankle joints causing the foot to fold very closely to the hips; then the thigh and knee are pulled forward and upward. The amount of knee lift is dependent upon the speed of the runner. Sprinters use a higher lift than middle distance runners because the lift is a result of a powerful drive of the foot and it puts the leg in a more desirable position for a longer stride length.

As the body continues to move forward, the leg begins to extend toward the ground. The ball of the foot again touches the ground.

ACTION OF THE FOOT

The feet, following the action of the legs, also move in a forward and backward direction. The toes should point straight ahead while the foot is on the ground. This will allow the thrusting action to direct its forces in the proper direction.

Contrary to walking, the ball of the foot touches the ground first, then as the weight of the body is transferred over the foot there is a momentary let down to the heel. The foot is then extended causing the weight to move forward over the ball of the foot.

Toeing-out in running puts the foot in a potentially weak position causing a reduction of the driving power. This may be noticed by checking foot prints around the track or observing the runner.

In general, a runner should run in a relatively straight line on the straightaway instead of weaving back and forth across the track and/or lane. When running around a curve, the runner should run as close as possible to the inside edge of the lane without stepping on or over the line. (See Figure 2).

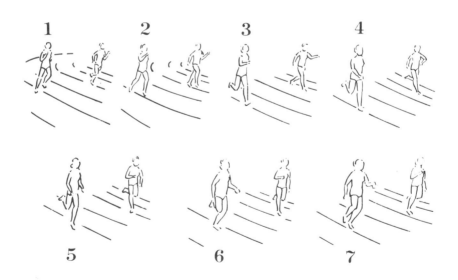

Figure 2. Running a curve

Chapter 4

TECHNIQUES OF SPRINTING
AND MIDDLE DISTANCE RUNNING

SPRINTING

Sprinting is generally referred to as running full speed over the entire distance. Distances up to 220 yards fall within the category. Being realistic, the longer sprint, such as the 220 yard dash, is run a fraction under full speed throughout the entire distance.

Sprinters come in all forms — some are tall with long strides and some are short and very explosive. Regardless of the body structure, there are some characteristics and qualities common to all sizes and shapes. Listed below are some of the most important qualities desired of a sprinter: (2)

1. Quick reaction time — possesses quick and efficient adjustment to a situation.
2. Quick reflex time — responds immediately to a stimulus.
3. Pure dominance — executes an efficient and definite sequence of movements.
4. Motor-mindedness — executes a sequence of movements without thinking about them.
5. Strong power of inhibition — possesses the ability to block out distractions.

STARTING

Types of Starts

There are two popular starting positions used by sprinters — one is the medium start and the other is the bunch start. The *medium start* is proported to put the runner into her running stride the fastest; while the *bunch start* will put the runner out of the starting position the fastest. Most of the experienced runners prefer to use the medium start because they realize that the one who is capable of getting into the running stride first is also capable of being in the best position to start accelerating into full stride. The bunch start is often referred to as the bullet start because of the manner in which it puts the runners out of the starting position. In fact, it will put them out so fast that they will find it necessary to make a momentary adjustment of the body before getting into the running stride. This momentary adjustment causes the loss of precious seconds.

Techniques of Starting

1. Determine which foot will be used as the forward foot in the starting position. This foot will be referred to as the *power foot* because it remains on the starting block the longest thereby permitting more power to be generated over a longer time from it. As a rule, right handed people use their left foot as the power foot and vice versa. One method of determining this foot is to stand erect with the body's weight equally distributed between the feet. Go through the motion of kicking a ball out of the hands. The foot which remains in contact with the ground is the power foot. This should be repeated several times to see if a consistent foot pattern develops.

2. *Bunch Start* (See Figure 3):

    Stand with back facing the direction of the run and measure two foot steps away from the starting line. Place a mark on the track. Turn around, then place the toe of the power foot on this mark. The toe of the other foot is placed approximately two inches opposite the heel of the power foot. (See Figure 4)

3. *Medium Start* (See Figure 5):

    Measure 1½ foot steps or two hand spans from the starting line; place a mark on the track. (See Figure 6) The toe of the power foot is placed on this mark. While the knee of the other leg is placed opposite the toe of the power foot.

4. *Elements common to both positions:* (See Figures 6 and 3a)

    The hands are placed up to, but not on or over, the starting line. They should form a high bridge with the thumbs separated from the other fingers. The fingers are held close together with most of the weight on the first and second fingers along with the thumbs.

    The arms, relatively straight, are placed shoulder width apart and the shoulders are over the hands.

    The head is in natural alignment with the shoulders and trunk. The eyes are focused on a spot approximately three feet in front of the starting line.

    The knee of the rear foot is on the ground. Both feet are resting against the starting block with just the toes in contact with the ground. The feet should be in line with the legs — that is, the heels and toes form a straight line with the legs.

Starting Commands

1. *"Take your mark."* Upon hearing this command, the runner, who was standing behind her starting blocks, walks in front of it and places her hands in front of the starting line. She backs

Figure 3a. Bunch start

Figure 3b. Bunch start — "set" position

Figure 4. Bunch start — placement of feet

Figure 5. Medium start

Figure 6. Medium start — placement of feet

Figure 7. Medium start — "set" position

into the blocks putting the forward foot in position then the other foot. Both feet are placed firmly against the blocks with only the toes touching the ground. If spikes are used, all of them should be placed firmly against the blocks. The hands are then moved into position behind the starting line. The shoulders are over the hands, while the arms are relatively straight; however, they are not hyper-extended. The eyes are focused approximately three feet ahead of the line. (See Figure 5.)

As soon as the runner is in position, she relaxes, takes a deep breath and concentrates on the next command.

2. *"Set."* When the command, "Set" is given she raises her hips until they are even with the shoulders or an inch or two higher than the shoulders. At the same time the body moves forward until the shoulders are two to three inches ahead of the hands. (See Figure 7)

The placement of the feet, as well as the length of the arms and legs will influence the height of the hips in this position. If the feet are too far from the starting line, the runner will have difficulty elevating her hips high enough. If the feet are too close to the line, there is a tendency to raise the hips too much. In either situation, a great deal of drive will be lost because the legs will not be in position to receive optimum power.

The eyes are still focused on a spot approximately three feet in front of the line. Any attempt to look farther down the track will put a strain on the neck. Also, it will encourage the runner to jump straight up when responding to the next command.

In the set position, the runner should concentrate on the gun or a loud noise. The concentration is so intense that any loud noise will cause a response. For this reason it is important for coaches and teachers to keep the area quiet while starts are being practiced or taken in a competitive situation.

Runners are held in the set position approximately 2.0 seconds, or until everyone is steady; however, the time may range from 1.5 to 2.0 seconds.

3. *"Go."* At the sound of the gun or some other loud noise, the runner drives out of the starting position. The first reaction is to *drive both feet* against the blocks. The force of this drive is observed in the first few steps. At the same time that the legs are driven against the blocks, both arms leave the ground. This is followed closely by a sequence of movements starting with

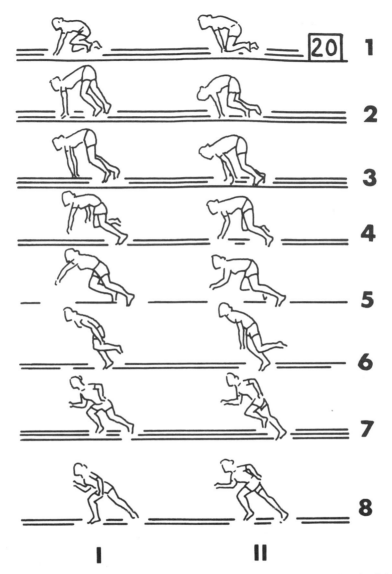

Figure 8. Sequence Action in Starting Position. Runner I (left): (1) runner is sitting too far back on her heels, also her shoulders are too far behind the hands; (2) the hips are relatively too high and the head is too high; (3-6) an upright position is assumed too soon. Runner II (right): (1) body's weight is forward, shoulders are just ahead of the hands; hips are slightly higher than the shoulders in the "set" position; (3-5) shoulders remain parallel to ground as the rear leg drives forward; (6-8) the trunk remains forward as the power foot drives forward.

the right leg assuming the left leg is forward in the starting position. Since there is an equal and opposite reaction to the drive against the block, the right leg drives forward along with a forward thrust of the left arm. The right arm moves in the opposite direction, so the arms, flexed at the elbow, should maintain angles close to 90 degrees. (See Figure 8) Throughout these movements the body is low and the shoulders are parallel to the ground.

The first stride is not a choppy step, instead, it is as long as possible without overstriding and destroying body balance. (See Figure 8) The trunk gradually assumes an upright position as the runner accelerates out of the blocks and into her full running stride. The first strides should be in a relatively straight line with each step slightly longer than the preceding one. Often runners will come out of the starting position off-balance stepping wide to each side. Naturally, this kind of action creates lateral motion which will weaken the forward drive.

Setting Starting Blocks

All starting blocks or holes should be set in the middle of their respective lanes in races that begin on the straight-away. The blocks should be set at an angle near the outside of the lane in races that start on a curve. This will help the runner to leave the starting position in a straight line instead of having to curve immediately. (See Figure 9)

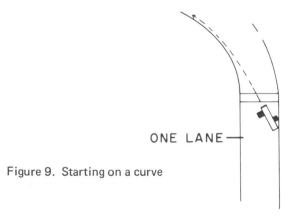

ONE LANE ⟶

Figure 9. Starting on a curve

THE RACE

Sprint Stride

The runner continues to accelerate as she leaves the starting position. By the time she has run 20 yards, she has assumed a relatively upright position of the trunk. Experienced sprinters will reach their maximum acceleration 50-60 yards from the starting line; however, novice and beginner runners will reach their maximum acceleration point within a much shorter distance such as 30-40 yards from the start.

Sprinters are smooth runners but they exhibit a tremendous amount of explosive power.

A sprinter's speed depends upon two factors — the length of the stride and the rate of the stride; therefore, the stride length of a sprinter is a little different from that of a middle distance runner.

Observe figure 10, notice the degree of relaxation and balance in the runner. These figures show the runner in the first few steps out of her blocks. Observe the lack of extraneous movements, such as lateral rotation of the trunk and toeing out. All of the forces and power are directed in the proper direction.

Figure 10. Running stride, sprinting

As the body rotates over the driving leg, it extends from the hip, knee, ankle, and foot; at the same time the other leg is moving into its recovery phase of the stride. The knee of the recovery leg is pulled *forward* and *upward* while the lower leg swings forward like a pendulum. The center of gravity is just ahead of the driving foot. The body continues to rotate forward (Figure 10). The hands and arms are relaxed moving in a forward and backward direction. The head is carried in an upright position with the eyes focused straight ahead and the jaws relaxed. Since sprinters reach their maximum acceleration 50-60 yards from the starting line, the runner who can maintain this maximum acceleration longest generally wins the race. Novice runners, unable to maintain this speed, tend to slow down the latter part of the race.

220 Yard Dash

In the 220 yard dash, the novice finds it difficult to maintain her maximum acceleration throughout the latter half of the race. She learns, instead, to distribute her speed throughout the distance. First, she accelerates for about 60 yards, then "floats" through the middle of the race, approximately 100 yards, ending with a drive through the last 60 yards. The float is described as maintaining a fast pace with relaxed hips and arms. It is difficult for an observer to notice this change but it is felt by the runner. As the girl becomes stronger as a result of training and/or conditioning, the floating period will be reduced. When running this distance around one curve, the girl will eventually learn how to pick up speed by lifting the knees higher in order to increase the length of her stride.

Figure 11. Running the curve, 200 m. U.S.-U.S.S.R. dual meet, 1964. Lane 1-Edith McGuire, U.S.A.; Lane 2-unidentified, U.S.S.R.; Lane 3-Vivian Brown. U.S.A.; Lane 4-Galine Popova, U.S.S.R.

Figure 12a. The finish

Figure 12b. The finish of a 440 yd. relay. W. Tyus, E. McGuire, M. White.

Eventually, she will learn how to accelerate through the first turn (110 yards) and to maintain this acceleration throughout the race. Outstanding sprinters like Wilma Rudolph and Edith McGuire learned to maintain their maximum acceleration over a long distance. This made it possible for them to run the 200 meters in 22.9 and 23.0 seconds.

The Finish

The runner should always think in terms of running through the tape instead of lunging at it. (See Figure 12) Experienced sprinters should learn to lean into the finish tape just in case of a close race. Often races are won by just a few extra inches received in a lean. The lean should occur in the last yard or two of the race. Through considerable practice, it can be taught to the girls.

MIDDLE DISTANCE RUNNING

440 Yard Run

In the 440 yard run *speed* as well as *pace* are important. Every day speed is becoming more important in the 440 yard run. While the distance used to be run in 59 and 60 seconds, top performers in the United States now cover it in 53 and 54 seconds. More sprinters are moving to the quarter mile because it is easier to increase strength and endurance to run this distance than it is to increase speed for the sprints when the sprinters may not have that extra quality needed for sprinting a shorter distance.

It is imperative for a girl to learn several important factors in order to effectively run the quarter mile. First, she must learn to relax. Mental as well as physical relaxation is emphasized to help her to run more smoothly. Second, she must learn to *judge* and *feel* running pace. Pacing is the product of *speed* and *stamina*. Since she cannot cover this distance at maximum speed, she must learn to pace herself so that she can distribute her efforts over the total distance. Third, she must continue to develop her sprinting ability. In order for her to run a faster race, she must increase her basic speed. Fourth, she must develop a positive attitude toward working hard in order to achieve success in this event.

Starting blocks should be used in 440 yard run because speed is relatively important. The runner, however, does not accelerate as fast as a sprinter.

The basic principles of running are the same as in sprinting with a few modifications. The arm actions are less vigorous because they are used for balance of the trunk as well as power, and the stride length is shorter because it is less demanding. The stride length should be natural. Overstriding is a common fault noticed among beginners when they are encouraged to increase the length of the running stride. This creates fatigue and also tends to retard the forward progress of the body.

After accelerating, the runner settles into a comfortable, yet fast, pace which is maintained throughout the race. Ideally, quarter milers should learn to run the second half of the race as fast as the first half; this is referred to as *even pacing*. At any rate, the split time between the two halves should not vary over two seconds. It is considered very poor strategy and a poor training technique to have a time difference of over three seconds between the two halves. Too much speed in the first half will leave the runner tired in the second half; while too little speed in the first part will allow the runner to finish with too much energy unused.

It is important for all quarter milers to learn how to run the curves properly. They should lean into the curves instead of being pulled away from them. (See Figure 11) If they are running in lanes, they should run close to the inside of their respective lanes without stepping on or over the line.

880 Yard Run

A great deal of improvement has been made in the half-mile within the last five years.

Again, the basic principles of running are followed in this distance; however, the actions of the arms and legs are reduced considerably. Individual differences in running style are noticed here more than in the previously mentioned distances. A girl's running style is basically inherited, therefore, it is the best style for her. Each one, however, would like to make her movements as efficient as possible because inefficient movements are readily noticed in the middle and long distances and these movements will create uneconomical and ineffective movements.

A shorter stride is used in this distance because it is more economical. A lower knee lift and less kick-up of the heels are needed because of the reduced power in the legs. The arms are relaxed and carried slightly lower than in the sprinting position. This carriage, however, may vary with each runner. As the runner drives for the finish, the entire action takes on the general characteristics of sprinting.

Stride length is very important in this distance. It should be natural and smooth (even). Overstriding and understriding are the most common faults in individual styles. Overstriding is the most serious of the two faults because of the energy wasted in the move-

Figure 13. U.S.-U.S.S.R. dual meet, 1964. U.S. runners — Sandy Knott (right) and Leah Bennett (left).

ment. If the stride is too short, it may be increased by developing more hip flexibility.

Since speed is not important, the runner should start in a standing position. Pace is important, therefore, the runner should learn the relationship between the individual fourths of the race (each 220 yards of the 880). Ideally, the quarters (220's) should be evenly paced but it doesn't always work out this way. If one works on the even-pace idea, however, a better race will eventually be run. The inability to judge pace is a common weakness among half milers. One way to overcome this weakness is to work with a watch. Some girls will learn to judge pace much faster than others. Eventually they will become pace conscious and will know the difference between a 30-32 seconds 220 and a 60-62 seconds quarter-mile.

Some runners run best from behind, others from being in front. Regardless of the place, they should learn to run their own race instead of following paces that are set too fast or too slow for them by others.

TABLE 3

OUTSTANDING PERFORMANCES IN THE U.S.A. IN THE 50 YDS.-50M. DASH

YEAR	50 YDS.	50 M.	NAME	AFFILIATION
1936		6.7	Ivy Wilson	Mercury A.C., N.Y.
1937		6.6	Claire Isicson	Eastern Women's Club
1938		6.4	Claire Isicson	Long Island Univ.
1941		6.6	Lucy Newell	Tuskegee Institute
1943		6.5	Alice Coachman	Tuskegee Institute
1944		6.4	Alice Coachman	Tuskegee Institute
1951		6.4	Mary McNabb	Tuskegee Institute
1952		6.4	Catherine Hardy	Ft. Valley State College, Ga.
1955	5.8		Isabel Daniels	Tennessee State
1956		6.4	Isabel F. Daniels	Tennessee State University Club
1958	5.7		Barbara Jones	Chicago, Ill.

TABLE 4

OUTSTANDING PERFORMANCES IN THE U.S.A. IN THE 100 YDS.-100 M. DASH

YEAR	100 Y.	100 M.	NAME	AFFILIATION
1935		11.6	Helen Stephens	Fulton (Mo.) H.S.
1938		12.4	Lula Hymes	Tuskegee Institute
1942		12.1	Alice Coachman	Tuskegee Institute
1943		11.6	Stella Walsh	Polish Olympic Women's A.C.
1945		12.0	Alice Coachman	Tuskegee Institute
1953		11.9	Barbara Jones	Chicago C.Y.O.
1955	10.7		Mae Faggs	Tennessee State
1956		11.7	Mae Faggs	Tennessee State University Club
1960	10.5		E. Pollard	Chicago MDYF
			E. McGuire	Tennessee State
1961		11.2	Wilma Rudolph	Tennessee State
1962	10.8		Wilma Rudolph	Tennessee State
1964		11.2	Wyomia Tyus	Tennessee State
1965	10.3	11.1	Wyomia Tyus	Tennessee State

TABLE 5

OUTSTANDING PERFORMANCES IN THE U.S.A. IN THE 220 YDS.-200 M. DASH

YEAR	220 Y.	200 M.	NAME	AFFILIATION
1935	24.3		Stella Walsh	Polish Olympic A.C.
1937		26.0	Gertrude Johnson	Mercury A.C., N.Y.
1939		25.5	Stella Walsh	Polish-American A.C.
1941		25.2	Jean Lane	Wilberforce University
1944		24.6	Stella Walsh	Unat., Cleveland
1945	26.3		Stella Walsh	Cleveland Polish Olympic W.A.C.
1949		24.2	Nell Jackson	Tuskegee Institute
1955	25.1		Mae Faggs	Tennessee State
1956		24.2	Wilma Rudolph	Tennessee State
1956		24.2	Mae Faggs	Tennessee State
1959		23.4	Lucinda Williams	Tennessee State
1962	24.1		Vivian Brown	Tennessee State
1964	23.4	23.0	Edith McGuire	Tennessee State
1964		22.9	Wilma Rudolph	Tennessee State

TABLE 6

OUTSTANDING PERFORMANCES IN THE U.S.A. IN THE 440 YD.-400 M. AND 880 YD.-800 M. RUN

YEAR	440 Y.	400 M.	NAME	AFFILIATION
1958		58.4	Lillian Green	N.Y. PAL.
1958	61.5		Chris McKenzie	
1964	54.8	54.5	Janell Smith	Kansas
1965		53.7	Janell Smith	Kansas
1966	53.3	53.0	Charlotte Cook	Los Angeles Mercurettes

YEAR	880 Y.	800 M.	NAME	AFFILIATION
1958		2:18.6	Lillian Green	N.Y. PAL.
1958	2:26.7		Flo McArdle	
1959		2:11.3	D. Lysenko-Shevlsova	U.S.S.R.
1963	2:11.7		Sandra Knott	Cleveland Rec.
1964		2:08.8	Leah B. Ferris	Hawaii
1965		2:07.3	Marie Mulder	Washington D.C.
1966	2:04.6	2:03.8	Charlotte Cook	Los Angeles, California

Running strategy should be carefully mapped out before the race. Some of the points each girl should consider are listed below:

1. Position in the race — decide if it is better to set the pace or follow the pace setter.
2. Follow the pace setter by maintaining physical and mental contact with her — approximately 15-20 yards.
3. Run off the shoulder of the person in front. Never allow other runners to "box you in."
4. Run the shortest distance possible by staying relatively close to the curb except when passing.
5. Pass a runner when going into the straight away, if at all possible. Be definite about the passing — pass quickly.
6. Entering the back-stretch (the last 150 yards), size up the situation and make a definite move.

Teaching Pace

Pacing is difficult for many girls to master because of the many factors which interfere with it. With self-discipline, however, it can easily be mastered.

Select a time that can be achieved easily in 220 yards — for example, 36 seconds. Divide this distance and time in half — two 110's (18 seconds each). Using two timers, stationed one at the 110 yard mark and the other at the 220 yard mark, run the 220 yards at a brisk pace — passing the 110 mark in 18 seconds. Allow one second difference on either side of the target time. If the runner is too fast or too slow, she should make an adjustment in the second half of the 220 yards. Repeat this several times. Gradually increase the distance to 440 yards.

SUMMARY OF RULES CONCERNING RUNNING (1, 3, 5)

1. Starting blocks may be used in track events, not as a material aid to the runner, but to protect the track.
2. Starting blocks may be used in races not exceeding 880 yards and in relay races by the lead-off runner.
3. In all races run around turns not in lanes, the starting line should be curved so that wherever it occurs on the track all of the runners can cover the same distance.
4. The direction of the runner should be left hand inside.
5. The finish (tape) is used as an *aid* to the judges. It is fastened to the finish post and it is parallel to the finish line on the track.
6. All competitors must run the full distance of their race. They must start with every part of their body, including hands and feet, behind the starting line. The finish is determined by the

order in which any part of their body (torso as distinguished from head, arms, legs or feet, but including the neck) reaches the finish line.

7. Any runner who willfully jostles, or runs across the path of another runner in order to force her to change her course, or impedes the progress of another runner is subject to disqualification.

8. Any competitor who in the opinion of the referee is being materially aided by another person during competition (running along side of, pacing, or coaching) may be disqualified.

9. Races run in lanes require each competitor to run the alloted distance in her own lane.

10. It is considered a false start if a competitor leaves her mark with hand or foot after the word "Set" but before the shot is fired. Two false starts will disqualify the runner. "Beating the Gun" is also considered a false start.

TRAINING HINTS FOR COMPETITION AND CLASS WORK

(NOTE: Reduce the number of repetitions for class.)

100 and 220 Yard Dash

Monday:
Warm-up: jogging and exercises
6 x 60 yards
Form work on starting – 20 min.
Practice passing baton – 15 min.
Finish with 220 (3/4 speed) then easy jogging on grass

Tuesday:
Warm-up: jogging and exercises
4 x 220 (7/8 speed)
10 starts with gun
Practice passing baton with relay
Finish with 150 (7/8 speed) then easy jogging on grass

Wednesday:
Warm-up: jogging and exercises
2 x 150; 2 x 100; 2 x 60
5-6 starts with gun
Finish with easy striding on grass

Thursday:
Warm-up: jogging and exercises
3 x 250

Practice passing baton, 3-4 exchanges top speed
Finish with easy jogging on grass

Friday: 4 x 150
Practice starts 6 x 40
4 x 80 (running curves)
Finish with easy jogging on grass

(NOTE: Work is designed to have two hard days and one light day.)

	440	*880*
Monday:	Warm-up Repeat 4 x 660 Finish with jog on grass	Warm-up 10 x 220 (walk 220 recovery) Finish with jog on grass
Tuesday:	Warm-up 6 x 330; back to back with jog between 4 x 60 Finish with jog on grass	Warm-up Fartlek - 5 miles
Wednesday:	Fartlek - 30 minutes	Warm-up 6 x 440 (walk 440 recovery) Finish with job on grass

Thursday:	Warm-up
	7 x 220
	3 x 110
	Practice starts 5 x 50
	Finish with jog on grass
		Warm-up
		2 x 3/4 mile (jog 3 laps be-
		  tween); repeat 2 more
		  times
		Finish with jog on grass

Friday:	Warm-up 2 x 60; 2 x 100; 2 x 150; 2 x 175 Finish with jog on grass	Warm-up 2 x 220; 2 x 330; 2 x 440; 2 x 220 distance run) Finish with jog on grass

BIBLIOGRAPHY

1. *A.A.U. Track and Field Handbook, 1965.* New York: The Amateur Athletic Union of the United States, pp. 137-140.
2. Breshnahan, G.T., W.W. Tuttle and F.X. Cretzmeyer, *Track and Field Athletics.* St. Louis: C.V. Mosby Company, 1964, p. 56.
3. *D.G.W.S. – Track and Field Guide, 1966-68.* Washington: Division of Girls and Women Sports.
4. Henry, Franklin M., "Force-Time Characteristics of the Sprint Start," *The Research Quarterly.* October, 1952, Vol. 23, No. 3, pp. 301-318.
5. *I.A.A.F. Handbook (English Edition), 1965/66.* London: International Amateur Athletic Federation, pp. 92-95.

Chapter 5

RELAY RACING

To many, relays are the most exciting events found in the track and field programs. Standard distances which may be included in a meet are as follows: (1) 220 yards (4 x 55); (2) 440 yards (4 x 110); (3) 880 yards (4 x 220); and (4) 880 yard sprint medley (220 - 110 - 110 - 440).

Relay teams consist of four runners, each one running a designated distance. In some relays, such as the 440, all runners cover the same distance — 4 x 110; however, in medley relays, like the 880 sprint medley, runners cover different distances — 220 - 110 - 110 - 440.

Races that are run around the oval are called *pursuit relays*. Those that are run back and forth over the same area are called *shuttle relays*. This discussion will be limited to techniques involving the pursuit relays.

In a pursuit relay the baton is passed from one runner to the next within a passing zone that is 22 yards long. Most of the governing organizations for track and field have adopted the international rule concerning the passing zone for sprint relays. In races up to 4 x 220 yards members of the team, other than the first runner, may start running 11 yards outside of the passing zone. A distinct mark should be made in each lane to denote this starting point. The baton must be passed within the passing zone.

The baton is generally passed from *left* to *right*: that is, the incoming runner carries it in her left hand and passes to the right hand of the outgoing runner. A right to left exchange is often used too. It is used to alternate with the left to right exchange when a runner receives the baton going into the curve.

Teamwork is very important to the four girls making up the relay team. Check marks are used to help the outgoing runner determine when she should start moving in order to receive the baton. The girl puts a check mark on the track in her lane (e.g. drawing a line across the lane) approximately five to seven yards to the rear of the passing zone or to the rear of the 11 yards behind the passing zone.

When the incoming runner passes this mark, the receiver starts sprinting from a semi-crouched position.

TYPES OF BATON EXCHANGE

There are two general classifications of baton exchange — the blind or nonvisual and the visual exchanges. The type of exchange used varies with the type of relay (over all distance of the relay). Regardless of the type of exchange, the basic problem remains the same — that of keeping the baton moving as fast as possible throughout the race including the passing zone.

The blind or nonvisual exchange is used in sprint relays such as the 440 and 880. This technique requires a great deal of practice and perfect timing. The incoming runner passes the baton to the outgoing runner who is looking forward in the direction of the run and accelerating toward top speed. Ideally, the exchange should take place within the last five yards of the passing zone. This will allow the outgoing runner to gain as much momentum as possible before receiving the baton. At the same time, the baton will be exchanged at a fast rate of speed. All things being equal, the momentum of both runners will bemaintained throughout the exchange.

TYPES OF BLIND OR NONVISUAL EXCHANGES

Underhand Exchange (See Figure 14): The outgoing runner extends her right arm to the rear with the palm facing diagonally down and back. The four fingers are together and extended while the thumb is abducted from the hand. A reverse "V" is formed by the separation of the thumb from the fingers.

Holding one end of the baton, the incoming runner carries it in her left hand. When she is in reaching distance of the receiver, she passes the baton with an upward and forward swinging motion of the arm. The baton is placed between the thumb and the first finger of the right hand. The incoming runner is expected to *reach forward* in order to complete the pass. As soon as the baton is received by the outgoing runner, she immediately transfers it to the other hand, grasping the baton near one end with three-fourths of it exposed on the thumb side of the hand.

This same technique may be used without changing hands upon receiving the baton. The runners use an *overlapping* hand grip as the baton is being exchanged; therefore, it is not necessary to transfer the baton from one hand to the other. The receiver keeps it in the right hand and executes a right to left exchange in the next zone.

Overhand Exchange (See Figure 15): The receiver extends the right arm backward and turns the palm up by flexing the wrist. The

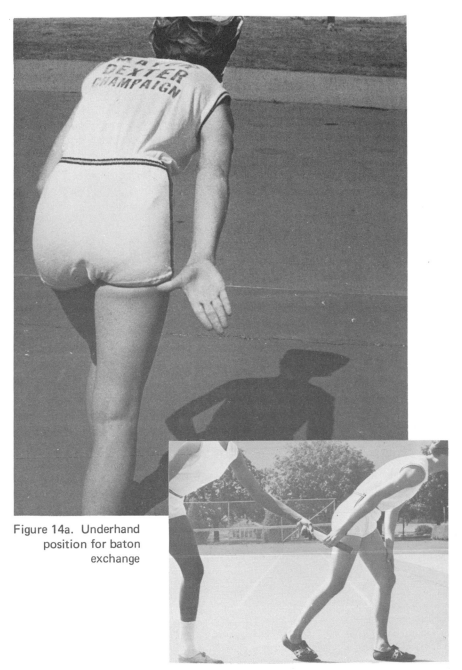

Figure 14a. Underhand position for baton exchange

Figure 14b. Baton exchange using underhand technique

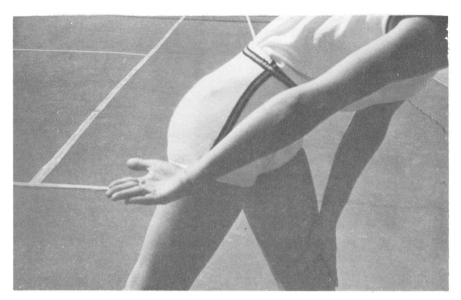

Figure 15a. Overhand position for baton exchange

Figure 15b. Baton exchange using the overhand technique

thumb is separated from the other fingers. With the baton in the left hand, the incoming runner swings the arm forward and downward placing the baton across the palm of the receiver's hand. The baton is placed in the hand so that the receiver is grasping one end of it. When the baton is pulled forward the girl is holding it in a manner that makes it unnecessary to transfer hands. She is ready for a right to left exchange.

Modification of the Two Techniques: A more advanced technique may be used by experienced runners. When the incoming runner reaches the check mark designated by the receiver, the outgoing runner starts moving using both arms as in sprinting to help her to accelerate faster. (See Figure 16) When the incoming runner gets close enough to pass the baton, she gives a verbal command, such as "Reach," the receiver responds by extending the right arm down and back. Either the underhand or overhand exchange may be used with this pumping action of the arms.

Figure 16. Spring pass exchange — R. Bonds to E. McGuire

THE VISUAL EXCHANGE

The visual exchange method of passing the baton is used in longer relays when the incoming runner is tired, uncertain of her speed and unable to judge the precision of hand-eye coordination. In these relays the receiver must keep her attention on the baton until it is placed in her hand. It is her responsibility to judge the speed of the incoming runner. If the incoming runner appears to be very tired, the baton should be passed in the rear half of the zone; however, if she appears to be relatively strong, the exchange should occur in the forward half of the zone. Unlike the sprint relays, the girl must start running within her passing zone.

During the exchange the receiver's speed should match that of the incoming runner. As the exchange occurs, the outgoing runner turns slightly to the right and extends her right arm back with the palm rotated up. The baton is placed across the palm with a downward swing of the left arm. As soon as the baton has been received, it is transferred to the other hand.

TEACHING HINTS (UNDERHAND TECHNIQUE)

1. Practice and recovery without baton:
    A. Divide the girls into groups of two's.

        Group 1:   X   X   X   X
        Group 2:   X   X   X   X

    B. Group 1 stands in a forward stride position with the right arm extending back. Group 2 stands two yards behind the other group and practices a forward thrusting action by touching the reversed "V" of the receiver's hand. This is repeated several times. Check often to see if the receiver's palm is facing the proper direction.
    C. Both groups turn around so that the girls in Group 1 can pass to Group 2. Repeat several times.
    D. Separate the groups five yards and walk through the pass. Repeat several times.
    E. Move the groups 10 yards apart. Draw a line between the groups – five yards behind Group 1 – to serve as a check mark.

        Group 1   ⎧ X   X   X   X   X
             10 yds.⎨ _____ Y (Teacher)
        Group 2   ⎩ X   X   X   X   X

        Group 1 observes their partners approach the check mark in a slow jog. When Group 2 reaches the mark, Group 1 starts jogging also. Group 2 passes to Group 1.
2. Practice thrust and recovery with baton:

A. Combine the groups so that four girls are in each group. Line them up — one behind the other — three yards apart. This time use a baton and practice the thrust, recovery, and baton transferance among the four girls.

B. Gradually widen the distance between the girls and have them jog, then run through the exchange at 1/2 and 3/4 efforts.

STRATEGY IN RUNNING RELAYS

1. For a left to right exchange, the receiver should start running on the left side of the lane. In a right to left exchange, she starts on the right side. This will allow the receiver to run relatively straight after receiving the baton and it will also leave room for both runners to use the lane without stepping on the line.

2. All runners should learn to slow down and remain in their respective lanes until all exchanges have been completed at their station.

3. If the relay starts on a curve, the starting blocks should be placed on an angle to permit a straight run into the curve.

4. The girl who starts the relay team should begin the race with the baton in the hand she plans to pass it in. The last girl on the team does not have to pass to anyone so she should run her distance with the baton in the receiving hand.

5. Runners differ in ability and temperment where team effort is concerned in running a relay. Individual characteristics should be remembered when palcing a girl on the team. It is not a simple matter of starting the second fastest runner and finishing with the fastest. It is wise to consider some of the following factors:

A. The ability to work together.

B. The ability to run the curves and straightaways. The long legged girls usually run the straightaway best and the shorter girls run the curves best.

C. The ability to give the team a good start.

D. The ability to run from behind, or to run strong if in front. Many girls lack that fighting spirit when they are behind — so they give up; others give up when passed in a race.

E. The ability to maintain a cool head during the race.

6. Place each girl in the best position according to her ability. Consider the overall distance each leg of the relay will cover. The first runner runs approximately 118 yards (110 plus eight into the receiver's area), second and third runners run their 110 yards plus 11 yards by starting in the rear of the passing zone and ap-

TABLE 7
OUTSTANDING PERFORMANCES IN THE U.S.A. IN THE 440 YD.-400 M. RELAY

YEAR	440 Y.	400 M.	NAME	AFFILIATION
1936		48.4		Illinois Catholic Women's Club
1946		49.4	C. Burge, J. Abbott, R. Harrison, L. Hymes	Tuskegee Institute
1942		50.7	L. Purifoy, L. Perry, R. Harrison, A. Coachman	Tuskegee Institute
1943		50.6		Toronto Laurel Ladies A.C.
1946	50.0		N. Mackay, R. Herrgan, V. Myro, S. Eckel	Malvernette A.C., Team A, Toronto
1947		50.5	M. Walker, J. Watson, M. Griggs, N. Jackson	Tuskegee Institute, Team A
1948		50.3	M. Walker, J. Watson, T. Manuel, N. Jackson	Tuskegee Institute, Team A
1949		50.0	N. Jackson, J. Lowe, T. Manuel, E. Hogan	Tuskegee Institute, Team A

Year	Time	Team	
1951	49.8	M. McNabb, C. Johnson, E. Lawler, N. Jackson	Tuskegee Institute, Team A
1953	49.7	H. Watkins, A. Lyman, B. Jones, M. Landry	C.Y.O., "A" Team
1954	49.0	H. Watkins, A. Lyman, M. Landry, B. Jones	Chicago C.Y.O., "A" Team
1955	49.1	M. Hudson, L. Williams, I. Daniels, M. Faggs	Tennessee State
1956	47.1	M. Hudson, W. Rudolph, I. Daniels, M. Faggs	Tennessee State Univ. Club, "A" Team
1957	47.0		Tennessee State Univ.
1959	44.8		U.S.S.R. National Team
1964	43.9		U.S.A. National Team
1965	44.3		U.S.A. National Team
1966	45.7		Tennessee State Univ.

proximately 8 yards into the next runner's area for a total distance of about 128 yards, and the fourth runner covers her 110 yards plus 11 yards by starting in the rear of her passing zone for a total of 121 yards.

For clarification of the above discussion, see Figure 17. The boundary lines of the passing zone (22 yards) extends 11 yards before and after the line which indicates 110 yards.

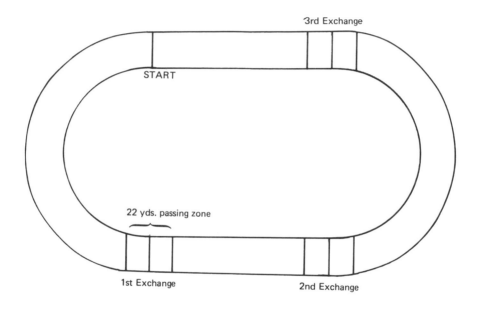

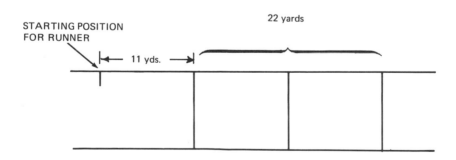

Figure 17. Passing zone for sprint relay

Chapter 6

CROSS COUNTRY

Cross country running is a wonderful conditioner for girls who are interested in middle distance and distance running. The maximum distance for girls in the United States is two miles. The IAAF (International Amateur Athletic Federation) permits girls to run distances up to two miles. Within the next few years this distance may increase another one-half or one mile. This assumption is made on two observations: 1) the increasing interest and participation of girls in the longer distances, and 2) the physiological implications indicate that women seem to be well suited to perform in sports activities which require endurance instead of those that demand high levels of strength or power. (1) However, for classroom purposes and novice groups, one-half, three-quarter, and one mile distances are often run.

Cross country is run over a terrain quite different from the track. It is usually mixed with rolling hills which require uphill and downhill running along with long stretches of flat terrain. One of the advantages of cross country, other than its conditioning factor, is that it allows for a change in scenery. This change will reduce boredom associated with running around the oval. The edges of golf courses are used by many school teams for this purpose.

A team usually consists of eight runners. In a meet, the first five runners of each team to cross the finish line will receive points for their teams. First place receives one point, second place two, and so on. The team score is determined by totaling the points scored by the first five members of each team to finish. If less than five members of a team finish, their team points will be disregarded.

RUNNING TECHNIQUE

Cross country running is important for those who run the sport competitively. It is more than a pleasurable jog, rather it is a gruelling, energy consuming run often performed under adverse weather conditions.

1. *Pace.*

Pacing is very important for this event. The general idea is to spread one's energy over the entire distance just as in the distance races on the track.

Figure 18a. Start of a cross country run

Figure 18b. Cross country running

It is important for the girls to feel their pace throughout the run in order to judge their speed. Since the terrain is always changing, they must be aware of the amount of output needed to cover the varying surfaces.

Teachers and coaches generally encourage their runners to stay together with a minimum difference in time between the first and last person in the group. This does not mean that those in front should wait for those who fall behind, instead the slower ones are encouraged to stay with the leaders.

To avoid losing mental contact or alertness with what is going on, the girls should quicken their pace for five or ten yards every quarter mile then settle back into their regular pace.

2. *The Hills.*

There are several techniques involved in running hills. When running downhill, the pull of gravity should be used advantageously. That is, the runners should take advantage of the momentum gained from the slope. A controlled, relaxed run should be utilized. The runner allows the slope to pull the body. Although the length of stride is mostly an individual matter, the steeper the hill the shorter the stride to insure proper footing. When running uphill, the following adjustments are made — 1) an increased forward body lean; 2) an increase in the pace; and 3) a slight increase in the length of the stride.

SCORING AND TIMING

1. A cross country team consists of eight girls unless it is otherwise agreed to change the number.

2. First place score is one point, second place score is two points, third place is three points, etc. The team score is determined by totaling the points scored by the first *five* members of each team. The team totaling the smallest score is the winner. If a team has less than five members to finish, their points are not added in the team scoring.

3. The final times of each runner should be recorded. One person calls the time at the finish while another records it. The timer calls the time as the runner passes the finish line. If a time chart is used, the recorder just places a mark at the reported time. A third person is stationed at the finish line to pass out place numbers as the runners cross the line. Later the numbers are collected and the names of the runners are placed on a sheet combined with the times.

COURSE MARKING

The course should be properly measured and marked. Generally, a lime-line outlines the entire course. In addition, flags or other markers are used to indicate the direction of turns — right or left.

FINISH CHUTE

The finish chute is used as a method of controlling the finish. Flags, boxes, benches, etc., may be used to indicate the chute. (See Figure 19)

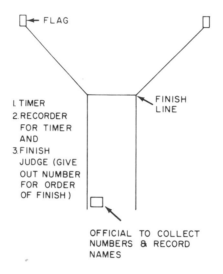

CROSS COUNTRY FINISH AREA

Figure 19. Finish shute — cross country

CONDITIONING

Conditioning for cross country is varied. A typical one day program would include:
1.   Jogging — one to two miles.
2.   Warm-up exercises.
3.   Sprinting uphill 7/8 speed six to eight times (the hill should have an incline of 110-220 yards).
4.   3 x 660
5.   One mile at race pace.

BIBLIOGRAPHY

1. Heusner, William W., *Basic Physiological Concepts as They Relate to Girls' Sports.* Second National Institute on Girls Sports: Washington: National Education Association, 1966.

Chapter 7

BASIC PRINCIPLES AND TECHNIQUES OF HURDLING

Good hurdlers must be good sprinters because three-fourths of the action in a hurdle race is sprinting.

Hurdling in its simplest form is a modification of sprinting, therefore the basic principles for running are applicable to hurdling (See Chapter II). The major concern of a hurdler is what is happening to the body while it is in the air and how can the body move as efficiently as possible while going over the hurdle.

It has already been pointed out that once the runner leaves the ground the flight course of her center of gravity has been determined, and it will remain undisturbed until contact has been made again with the ground.

There are several forces acting upon the body as it rotates in several planes over the hurdle. There is simultaneous body rotation in three planes — horizontal, frontal, and sagittal as the rear leg pulls through and the lead leg cuts down to the ground. Geoffrey Dyson explains that "in the horizontal plane, the action of the hurdler's lower limbs twists his upper body toward the trailing leg; in the frontal plane, it also tilts it down in the direction of this leg; and in a sagittal plane, the reaction rotates him backward as in the hitch-kick. In all three planes, a clockwise motion produces simultaneous counter-clockwise reaction and vice versa; in each case angular momenta are equal but opposite."(1)

HURDLE CLEARANCE

The key to efficient hurdling lies in the relationship of the hurdler's center of gravity to the top of the hurdle. There are several factors which should be realized in order to understand this relationship.

1. *Speed of the Approach.*

The faster the approach speed the closer the center of gravity will come to the top of the hurdle. A fast approach permits the take-off to be started farther away from the hurdle thereby causing the high point of the flight path of the center of gravity of the hurdler to occur approximately one to two feet on the approach side of the hurdle. The hurdle should be cleared at maximum horizontal speed.

2.   *Clearance.*

In order for the lead leg to clear the hurdle efficiently, the take-off spot should be established far enough from the hurdle to allow a good split or stretch to occur between the lead leg and the rear leg. At the same time the trunk is bent slightly forward to keep the center of gravity ahead of the driving foot and to reduce the amount of backward rotation. The distance between the take-off and the hurdle is greater than the distance between the hurdle and the landing.

The movement over the hurdle is a fast pivotal action of the legs. The lead leg pulls up with the thigh leading, followed by an extension of the lower leg toward the top of the hurdle. The rear leg folds to the side and swings laterally over the hurdle top. As soon as the heel of the lead leg crosses the hurdle, it starts cutting down to the ground while the rear leg continues to pivot over the top. The quick action of the leg will limit the amount of time spent in the air. The landing should be smooth and balanced so that the hurdler can "sprint off the hurdle."

The legs are moving continuously throughout the clearance. The action is so timed that there is good cadence between the lead leg and the rear leg. If the rear leg pivots into action too soon it will rush the lead leg, causing it to land slightly behind the center of gravity instead of slightly in front of it. The first stride which is taken with the rear leg will be very short and it throws the body off balance.

An effective and efficient movement of the lead leg depends to a great extent upon the timing of the rear leg. A delayed action of the leg, therefore, will give a faster and more continuous movement of the rear leg, which in turn influences good timing and speed upon touching the ground.

As mentioned earlier, there is considerable rotation as the body moves through the air. Dyson [1] indicated that these movements may be absorbed in the following manner:

1.   In the horizontal plane — by holding the forward lean to increase the horizontal distance between the axis of displacement (an axis parallel to the body's center of gravity) and the secondary axis of the shoulder. (Motion of a part of the body about an axis at a distance to the center of gravity.)

2.   In the frontal plane — by lowering and extending the opposite arm in its backward swing while simultaneously raising the other arm, thus preventing an exaggerated upper-body tilt toward the rear leg.

TECHNIQUES OF HURDLING

The height of the hurdle that is used by girls is two feet six inches. Contrary to boys, girls use only one size as their official height; however, they have several hurdling events available to them. These distances are listed below.

Distance of Race	Number of Hurdles	Distance From Start to 1st Hurdle	Distance Between Hurdles	Distance From Last Hurdle to Finish
50 yards	4	39'4½"	26'3"	31'10½"
60 yards	5	39'4½"	26'3"	35'7½"
70 yards	6	39'4½"	26'3"	45'9"
50 meters	4	39'4½"	26'3"	39'4½"
80 meters (87½ yards)	8	39'4½"	26'3"	39'4½"
100 meters	10	13 m.	8.5 m.	10.5 m.
200 meters	10	28 m.	16 m.	28 m.

There are two general styles of hurdling. One emphasizes a straight lead leg with a forward lean of the trunk, and the other emphasizes a partially bent leg with a relatively upright position of the trunk. Often the size of the hurdler will determine the style to be used. Girls who have long legs generally use the partially bent lead leg, while those with shorter legs will tend to use the relatively straight lead leg. Sometimes a combination of the two styles is used.

The leg that goes over the hurdle first is referred to as the *lead* leg. The other one is referred to as the *trailing* or *rear* leg.

1. *Action of the Lead Leg.*

When the runner approaches the hurdle, the knee of the lead leg is pulled up toward the chest until the heel of the lower leg is level with the top of the hurdle. The leg is then extended forward with the heel leading the action. (See Figure 20). The foot and leg skim over the top of the hurdle. As the momentum of the body carries the leg over the hurdle, it is snapped down relatively close to the far side of the hurdle. In landing, the weight is taken in the ball of the foot.

The hurdler takes-off far enough from the hurdle so that the lead leg has an opportunity to swing forward without noticeably altering the height of the center of gravity or the height of the girl's head as she goes over the hurdle. This is often referred to as having a good split between the lead and rear legs.

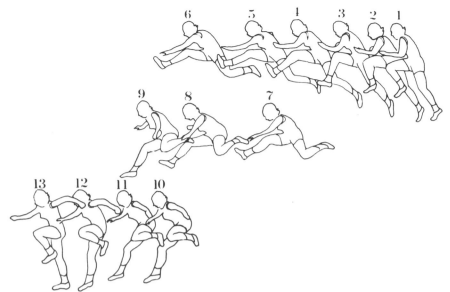

Figure 20. Sequence action of hurdling

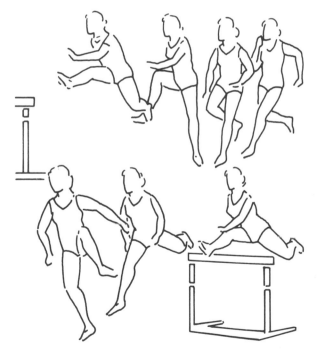

Figure 21. Hurdling — front approach

Figure 22. Action of arms, trunk and legs over hurdle. Cherrie Sherrard, top U.S. hurdler, 1966.

2.   *Action of the Rear Leg.*

While the lead leg is extending itself forward over the hurdle, the rear leg is left behind as long as possible. (See Figure 20) This delayed action of the rear leg is to encourage a wide split between the legs so the hurdler will skim very close to the top of the hurdle. The rear leg, in a continuous motion, is pulled forward over the hurdle with the inside of the leg passing next to the hurdle. The leg is flexed as it pulls in close to the body. The inside of the leg and foot pass over the hurdle in a relatively flat position. The foot is held in a flexed position with the inside of it parallel to the top of the hurdle to prevent the toes from catching the top of the hurdle. (See Figure 21)

After the lead leg touches the ground, the rear leg continues to pivot around the hurdle. The knee is pulled up toward the chest in order to place the leg in a good position to drive forward. (See Figure 20) The rear leg should reach forward and out as it comes over the hurdle because it takes the first full stride forward. If that first step is too short, the hurdler will have difficulty covering the distance between the hurdles.

3.   *The Action of the Arms and Trunk.*

The trunk moves ahead of the supporting foot as the thigh of the lead leg is pulled toward the chest during the take-off (See Figure 20) The arms, a bit exaggerated, are raised as in sprinting, that is, to balance the trunk and to prevent lateral rotation of it. If the left leg is leading over the hurdle, the right shoulder and arm will also be

Figure 23. Excellent position of lead and trail leg upon landing. Notice the position of the knee and foot of trailing leg.

pulled forward while the opposite arm is flexed at the elbow, moving toward the rear. (See Figure 22)

4.   *Landing.*

The lead leg touches the ground approximately two feet from the hurdle. The foot should be pointed straight ahead when it touches the ground. The rear leg takes the first full step; therefore, it should be a full running stride. Learning to sprint off the hurdle will help to gain speed between hurdles rather than lose it because of the obstacle.

THE START AND STRIDING BETWEEN HURDLES

Hurdlers, as a rule, are expected to use the same type of start that is used by sprinters because they want to accelerate as quickly as possible into their sprinting stride. Usually, seven, eight, or nine strides are taken to the first hurdle in distances up to and including the 80 meters. If the *left* leg is the forward leg in the starting position and it is also the *lead* leg over the hurdle, seven or nine strides are used, depending upon the length of the strides. (See Figure 24) Using the same starting position, left leg forward, but leading over the hurdle with the *right* leg, eight strides are needed to reach the first hurdle.

The following chart is a convenience guide for a striding plan.

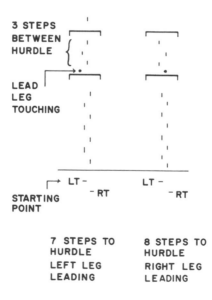

Figure 24. Stride plan for hurdling

TECHNIQUES OF BEGINNING HURDLING

A girl learning the skills of hurdling should move through a progression of skills in order that she may perform and understand the movements.

1. A relatively low barrier is placed across the track. This barrier may be a jump rope or a stick that is placed on some bricks. It is approximately eight inches high. Starting approximately 10 yards from the barrier, the girls should run over the barrier without altering their running pattern. Emphasis is placed on picking the knees up in front of the body during the run. The teacher should learn to identify by sound an even step pattern in the approach. This will help her to recognize and identify those girls who jump over the low barrier instead of running over it.

2. Gradually increase the height of the barrier to 12, 15, 18, and eventually 20 inches. As the barrier is raised, the girls will be faced with the need to lift their knees as well as to lengthen their strides. If the legs are lifted properly, the overall height of the body's center of gravity will not vary. Again, it is imperative that this movement be accomplished before moving to the next step. Often, beginners have a tendency to lift the entire body over the barrier in the form of a jump instead of lifting and stretching mainly the legs.

3. As the barrier is raised, the rear leg begins to assume the hurdling form. The knee of this leg rotates to the side while the lower leg folds sideways and pivots over the barrier.

4. One of the major problems encountered by beginner hurdlers is learning how to pivot the trail leg over the hurdle. One way of understanding this movement is to have the girls stand close to the side of the hurdle with the lead foot about three inches in front of it. An assistant is standing in front of the hurdle facing the girl. Using the left leg as the lead leg, the hurdler places her right hand on the shoulder of the assistant for balance. The assistant helps the hurdler with the rear leg by placing her hand under the knee and foot to support and guide the leg in the proper direction. When the foot has cleared the hurdle, the assistant guides the leg so that the knee will rotate up with the foot swinging forward and away from the hurdle. This is repeated several times.

5. The hurdlers walk along the side of the hurdle concentrating on placing the lead leg in front of it and swinging the rear leg over the hurdle without hesitating over the top of it.

Figure 25 a. Variety of forms in a hurdling race.

Figure 25b. Variety of hurdling forms. The girl in Lane 1 is using a bent lead leg while the one in Lane 3 is using a straight leg.

6. Gradually add a jog to the above practice. The success of this skill depends upon placing the lead leg a sufficient distance in front of the hurdle in order to eliminate an unnecessary hop over it.

7. Walk up to the center of the hurdle, pull the lead leg toward the chest and step over it, the rear leg pulls through as the lead leg touches the ground. Keep the shoulders and hips forward. Do not allow them to twist to either side; however, the hands may be used for balance on the hurdle.

8. Draw a line about three feet from the hurdle on the approach side. Jog toward it. When the runner reaches the line she should start taking off. This line should serve only as a guide to prevent the runner from taking off too near the hurdle. It should be gradually moved farther away from the hurdle as the group gains more self-confidence in their ability.

9. As soon as the form over one hurdle is under control, a second one should be placed approximately 20 feet ahead of the first one. The girls should be encouraged to run over this first hurdle, take three strides, and run over the second one. Since the distance between the hurdles has been shortened from 26 feet three inches to 20 feet, they should be able to cover the distance without any trouble. As soon as possible, the hurdle should be gradually moved to 26 feet three inches.

HINTS ON HURDLING

1. Hurdling is sprinting, therefore hurdlers should sprint up to the hurdle and off of it.

2. Speed is gained by being on the ground, not in the air, therefore hurdlers should not "float" over the hurdle. Instead they should skim as close to it as feasible.

3. As soon as the heel of the lead leg clears the hurdle, start cutting it toward the ground to eliminate unnecessary floating.

4. Good hurdling depends upon a good split between the lead and rear leg.

5. As far as possible, keep the shoulders and hips parallel to the top of the hurdle.

6. If the runners stride is too short, work toward developing more hip flexibility.

7. Overstriding between the hurdles should be discouraged because it will slow down the speed.

8. A single arm thrust is used over the hurdle. The action is in a forward and backward line with as little lateral motion as possible.

TABLE 8
OUTSTANDING PERFORMANCES IN THE U.S.A. IN THE 80 M. HURDLES

YEAR	80 M.	NAME	AFFILIATION
1936	11.8	Simone Schaller	
1937	12.7	Cora C. Gaines	Tuskegee Institute
1939	12.5	Marie Cotrell	German-American A.C., N.Y.
1943	12.3	Nancy Cooperthwaite	German-American A.C., N.Y.
1946	12.2	Nancy Cooperthwaite	German-American A.C., N.Y.
1948	12.1	Bernice Robinson	Washington Park, Chicago
1950	11.9	Evelyn Lawler	Tuskegee Institute
1952	11.8	Constance Darnowski	German-American A.C.
1955	11.5	Bertha Diaz	Cuba
1956	11.1	Bertha Diaz	Cuba
1957	12.4	Shirley Crowder	Tennessee State Univ.
1959	11.4	Barbara Mueller	Chicago C.Y.O.

1959	11.0	Gabina Grinwald	U.S.S.R.-National Team
1962	11.3	Cherrie Sherrard	San Francisco, Calif.
1962	10.7	Irina Press	U.S.S.R.-National Team
1964	10.8	Rosie Bonds	Los Angeles
1966	10.7	Cherrie Sherrard	San Francisco, Calif.

TABLE 8

OUTSTANDING PERFORMANCES IN THE U.S.A. IN THE 80 M. HURDLES

YEAR	50 M.	50 YD.	NAME	AFFILIATION
1955		7.0	Jeanette Cantrell	Tuskegee Institute
1956	7.8		Shirley Crowder	Tuskegee Institute
1966		6.5	Denise Paschal	San Francisco, Calif.

9.   The rear leg should not be rushed into action too soon because it will cause the hurdler to land with her feet too close together. This will make it difficult for her to cover the official distance between the hurdles in three strides. It will also throw her off balance upon landing.
10.   The trunk should remain ahead of the rear leg during the flight over the hurdle. If it is back too far or too upright, it will cause the girl to sit on top of the hurdle as she crosses it.
11.   The foot of the rear leg should remain flexed to the side as it crosses the hurdle to prevent the possibility of tripping over it.
12.   In a race, the girl should accelerate up to the fifth hurdle instead of the first one.

SUGGESTED WORK SCHEDULE FOR HURDLERS

1.   Generally, hurdlers should follow a program similar to sprinters.
2.   Special emphasis is given to exercises for flexibility such as the hurdle stretch, trunk bending, and circling of rear leg.
3.   Practice hurdle clearance over one, two, and three hurdles. Record the time it takes to cover the distance to each hurdle.
4.   Sprint over distances such as 100 yard for 80 m., 150 yards for 100 m., etc.

SUMMARY OF THE RULES CONCERNING HURDLING

1.   The general rules of running are applicable to hurdling.
2.   A runner should be disqualified if a) she trails a leg or foot along side of a hurdle; b) jumps a hurdle in another lane; or c) *deliberately* knocks over a hurdle with her hands.
3.   Unintentionally knocking down a hurdle will not disqualify a runner.

SUMMARY OF HURDLING ERRORS AND THEIR CORRECTION

1.   *Inadequate forward lean of the trunk.*
       This may be due to a) taking off too close to the hurdle; b) clearing it too high; or c) improper timing of the rear leg. If the take off is too close to the hurdle, a guide line should be drawn on the track one to two feet behind the previous take off spot. When traveling at a brisk pace, there is less difficulty in taking off an adequate distance from the hurdle. If there is not sufficient distance for the lead leg to extend forward at take off, the hurdler will find herself jumping in order to clear it. A slightly backward rotation of the trunk may be caused by improper swinging and timing of the trailing leg.
2.   *Faulty action of the rear leg.*
       In addition to the above error concerning improper timing, beginners often fail to raise the knee sufficiently to clear the cross piece.

They also have difficulty keeping the foot flexed to the side to prevent it from catching the cross piece. Improving the amount of flexibility in the hips and legs will help the girls to become more mobile. Also constant practice pivoting the rear leg over the side of the hurdle will correct this fault.

3.   *Faulty action of the lead leg.*

The failure to use the lead leg properly in an extended or partilly extended position will force the hurdler to clear the hurdle much higher than is necessary. The knee should be lifted first, followed by an extension of the lower leg The heel is directed toward the top of the hurdle forming a straight line of the leg from the hip. If the foot turns in or out as the leg extends forward because the take off is too close, the hurdler will again find herself floating over the hurdle and it will affect the balance of the body.

4.   *Faulty action of the arms.*

Good opposition action of the arms will contribute to good balance and a good lean of the trunk. A single arm thrust is better than a double arm thrust. Improper use of the opposition action will allow the trunk to twist laterally as the body crosses the hurdle. The arm opposite to the lead leg should be extended in a forward direction when the leg is extended. The other arm is carried backward.

Good action of the arms will also keep the shoulders and hips parallel to the hurdle.

5.   *A short first stride after clearning the hurdle.*

A short stride is usually the result of poor timing of the rear leg and poor balance over the hurdle. These errors cause the foot to be placed on the ground too soon. The regular stride length should be measured so the hurdler will be aware of the length of stride needed on the first step. Also a slight delayed action of rear leg will improve the timing and balance.

HURDLE EXERCISES TO LOOSEN AND STRETCH THE MUSCLES OF THE HIPS, LEGS, AND BACK

FIGURE 26

a. Hurdle stretch (seated).

b. Place lead foot on the hurdle, holding it with both hands. Bounce forward toward the extended foot.

c. Place the trail leg on the hurdle so that the knee and foot are resting on it. Bounce forward to touch the ground with both hands.

d. The rear leg is placed in the same position as "c". Bounce forward and backward.

BIBLIOGRAPHY

1. Dyson, Geoffrey, *The Mechanics of Athletics*. London: University of London Press LTD, 1963, pp. 119-120.

Chapter 8

BASIC PRINCIPLE
OF HIGH JUMPING

High jumping is a vertical jump over an obstacle which is usually a triangular shaped cross bar supported by two standards. The higher the jump, the more economical the style to be used by the jumper.

The effectiveness of the vertical jump depends upon two factors — *spring* and *lay-out*. Both of these are influenced by the runner's *approach* to the bar.

Geoffrey Dyson [2] said spring can account for approximately 90 per cent of the height obtained in a jump. He also stated that maximum efficiency in spring and/or lay-out can be obtained only at the expense of one or the other. In other words, the jumper must make a compromise between the spring and lay-out in order to be economically efficient. "To obtain economy of lay-out good jumpers drive eccentrically at take off, slightly reducing the effective spring, but in the process gain more through the position over the bar." [2]

THE APPROACH

The angle and speed of the approach influences the combined forces of take off and lay-out position of the jumper in the air.

Ideally, the *angle* of approach should be about 45 degrees to the cross bar; however, an approach of 30 - 40 degrees may be more economical for a straddle roll. At any rate, there are several advantages to approaching from an angle instead of head-on in front of the bar. Some of the advantages are listed below: 1) it allows the lead leg greater range through which it can swing during take off; 2) it allows some part of the body to be above and below the bar before the center of gravity reaches its highest point; 3) it allows the jumper to smoothly convert the momentum of the approach into an upward lift.

The amount of *speed* needed in the approach varies with the jumper; however, in general terms, she needs enough speed to carry the body over the bar. The amount of speed varies with such factors as 1) the height of the bar; 2) the angle of the approach, and 3) the ability to convert the horizontal momentum of the run into an upward vertical drive.

As the jumper approaches the bar, the last two or three strides are progressively longer than the preceding ones. This action places the take off foot just ahead of the body's center of gravity which creates a slightly backward rotation of the trunk. It also braces the body against its horizontal momentum, thereby allowing time for the free leg and arms to assist in the upward lift of the thrust from the supportive leg.

TAKE OFF

The take off phase of the high jump is a combination of converting horizontal momentum into a vertical lift. The jumper is faced with the responsibility of imparting maximum vertical velocity to her center of gravity and at the same time acquiring a sufficient amount of body rotation (i.e., total angular momentum) for her layout. [2]

The arms and legs contribute to the vertical velocity of the jump. As the knee of the take off leg bends during take off, the body's center of gravity is lowered and, as mentioned earlier, it is well behind the take off foot. This position causes the heel to drop to the ground. This settling action of the hips and leg compresses the body like a coil of springs. It places the leg muscles into a position whereby they can uncoil most effectively. [1] Because of the lower hip position, the free leg is unable to swing through in an extended position. It is partially bent at the knee, otherwise the foot will drag the ground.

Ideally, the lead leg should swing upward with vertical force just before the take off leg extends and exerts its force against the ground. The more extended the lead leg, all things being equal, the greater the force it can exert on the upward drive of the body. However, the more extended the leg, the greater its inertia, and the slower it is driven upward. [1]

The arms are used for balance and they contribute to the vertical lift by moving at maximum vertical speed during take off.

When the jumper leaves the ground as a result of the driving action of the arms and legs, her center of gravity should be projected from the greatest possible height. [2] This is accomplished by extending the trunk vertically along with the arms and legs.

Body rotation around the bar originates in many instances from the ground. The more the knee of the lead leg is bent on take off, the more body rotation is observed during this movement. Dyson [2] states that a constant total angular momentum is developed on each jump by checking the linear motion (through momentarily fixing the take off foot), transferring angular momentum (from the arms and legs), and by thrusting eccentrically to the center of gravity (with the jumping leg).

CLEARANCE

When contact with the ground has been broken during the jump, the flight path of the jumper's center of gravity is determined as far as direction and height are concerned. Because of this, the straddle roll is a much more efficient style of jumping than the scissors, provided the approach and vertical lift with both styles are with equal momentum and upward drive.

It is relatively easy to visualize the difference in body positions in the scissors and Western or straddle roll. The one constant factor that is common to the three styles is the *high point* of her center of gravity because of the amount of body surface above and below it. The height of the center of gravity may be five feet above the ground; however, the girl is capable of clearing only four feet because of the amount of body surface (the hips) below the weight center. Whereas, in the straddle roll, she is capable of clearing the bar very close to the high point of her center of gravity because of the reduced amount of body surface between the center of gravity and the bar. Therefore, the straddle roll is much more efficient and economical style than the scissors or Western roll. Actually, in the dive-straddle roll, a girl may be capable of clearing the bar at a slightly higher height than in a straight lay-out over the bar because of her ability to get some parts of the body over the bar, such as the arms, head, and shoulders, before the hips and take off leg have reached their high points.

The jumper finds it possible to jump higher by changing the position of her body in relation to her center of gravity while in the air. Any movement which originates in the air will cause an equal and opposite reaction within the body. (2) Therefore, those who use the straddle or Western roll drop their arms, head, and shoulders toward the landing pit as they cross the bar in order to assist the lower part of the body across.

BIBLIOGRAPHY

1.   Doherty, J. Kenneth, *Modern Track and Field*. Englewood Cliffs: Prentice-Hall, Inc., Second Edition, 1963, page 449.
2.   Dyson, Geoffrey, *The Mechanics of Athletics*. London: University of London Press LTD, 1963, pages 126-130.

Chapter 9

TECHNIQUES OF HIGH JUMPING

Today the most efficient manner of clearing the cross bar is by rolling over it. As mentioned in the preceding chapter, rolling over the bar is efficient because it enables the jumper to lay-out parallel to the bar with a minimum amount of body surface between the jumper's center of gravity and the bar and at the same time rotate her body around it.

There are two basic styles of jumping: 1) the Western roll and 2) the straddle roll. Except for the manner of clearance and landing, the two styles are relatively similar in the approach and take off.

Western Roll (See Figure 27)

In the Western roll, the take off is made with the foot nearest the cross-bar. In this style, clearance is made with the side of the body next to the bar.

Figure 27. Western roll. The bar would follow the path of the spine. The take-off leg is tucked close to the chest.

As the jumper leaves the ground, the lead leg, head, and arms will cross the bar first while the take off leg is pulled up under the lead leg. This leg is pulled very tight into the body with the knee close to the chest.

As the arms, head, and shoulders cross the bar they are immediately dropped toward the landing pit. The dropping of the above parts aids in clearance of the hips over the bar because the hips are pushed up and away from it.

The landing is made on the take off foot and both hands. The knee, wrists, and elbows flex as the body's weight is received upon these parts in order to ease the impact of landing.

Straddle Roll (See Figure 28)

The leg nearest the cross-bar is also used as the take off leg in the straddle roll; however, the body rotates around the bar in a face down position.

During the take off, the foot of the lead leg swings as high as the cross-bar before the supporting foot leaves the ground, at the same time the arms swing up in order to contribute to the explosive lift of the body. At the height of the jump the outside arm reaches across the bar toward the pit. The head and shoulders follow the path of this arm by dropping toward the pit (See Figure 28 8-9)

The legs remain separated as the body rotates around the bar. In fact, a "V" is formed between them during this action. In order for the take off leg to clear the bar, the knee and foot are rotated away from the bar, or they are extended up and back.

If a sawdust pit is used, a three point landing is recommended. The impact is taken on both hands and the lead leg; however, if the jumper is landing in a foam rubber pit, she should learn to land on her back or side by slowly rotating her head to look at the sky just after crossing the bar. This movement of the head creates a turning effect with the body.

THE APPROACH

The jumper approaches from the left side of the cross-bar if springing from the left foot, or right side if springing from the right foot.

Generally, the approach is long enough to allow the jumper to gather sufficient speed to clear the bar and at the same time have maximum control of the limbs during take off. This is usually accomplished with five to eight strides. Since speed is not a prime factor, a long, fast run is not recommended.

Most of the approaches are relatively slow; this is considered best. If the approach is too fast, the jumper will have difficulty trans-

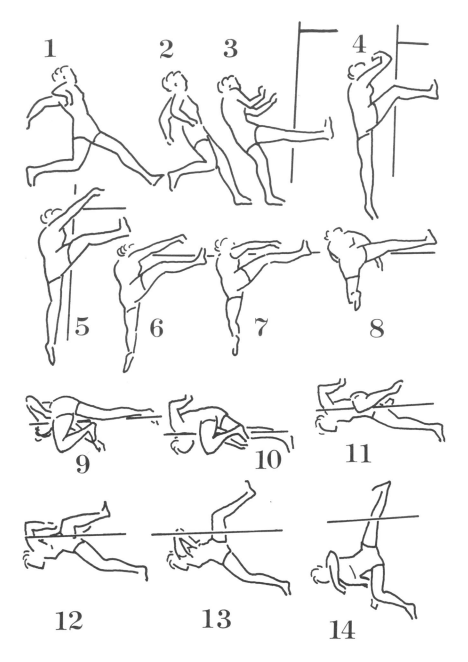

Figure 28. Straddle roll

ferring the direction of the forward momentum into a vertical lift.

The approach is made from a 30-45 degree angle to the bar. The specific angle varies with each jumper. Beginners should start with a 45 degree angle, as they develop in skill, a narrower angle may be assumed. Some of the better jumpers use an angle of 30-40 degrees. If a small angle is used, such as 30 - 35 degrees, the jumper's approach is more parallel to the bar, making it easier to get the body closer to the bar and to extend the lead leg straight ahead of the body during take off. At the same time, it is difficult for the jumper to get a good vertical lift because there is a tendency to travel down the bar which may be associated with diving. A 40 - 45 degree angle permits a more perpendicular approach and a vertical lift; however, this angle makes it difficult for the jumper to get close to the bar and at the same time extend the lead leg up and straight ahead of the body during the take off.

The last three strides to the bar are progressively longer than the other ones. This action tends to prepare the jumper for the take off. The knees bend, dropping the body into a slightly crouched position. On the last stride the take off foot reaches forward placing the center of gravity just behind the hips and in front of the trunk in order to enable the jumper to get a good backward lean and a long swing of the lead leg. The backward lean is fundamental to a good take off because it *starts* the body into a lay-out position.

THE TAKE OFF (See Figure 28 1-5)

The take off spot should be approximately an arm's distance from the center of the cross-bar. This spot may vary a little but not too much.

On the last stride of the approach, the inside foot is planted ahead of the center of gravity, heel first. The eyes are focused above the bar. The knee bends to gather for the vertical lift. As the lead leg swings forward and up, the body rotates over the take off foot. The jumper springs upward as the take off leg extends and pushes the body off the ground as high as possible.

The arms, particularly the outside one, drive upward along with an extension of the trunk. (Figure 28 4-5)

As the weight is transferred over the ball of the foot, the free leg swings up vigorously. It may be partially bent or relatively extended to assist with the upward thrust and beginning layout position. As pointed out earlier in the chapter on Mechanical Principles of High Jumping, a partially bent leg creates a vertical force that carries the body forward as well as upward, whereas a relatively extended leg drives the body vertically without the forward movement.

Figure 29. Straddle roll. A relatively straight layout over the bar. The head and shoulders are dropped toward the pit as soon as they cross the bar.

Actually, the take off is a combination of *kicking* then *springing,* instead of springing then kicking. In order to gain maximum spring and layout, timing of the combined movement, kicking and springing, is very important.

COMMON ERRORS IN HIGH JUMPING

1. Using an approach that is too long or too short. If the approach is too long the jumper will be tired when she reaches the bar; however, the run should be long enough to allow her time to build up sufficient speed. If the approach is too short, she will have difficulty getting a good vertical lift.
2. Springing, then kicking. This will drastically reduce the amount of vertical lift. Remember, it should be a kick then spring during take off.
3. Leaning into the bar with the inside shoulder during the take off. This may be caused by turning the shoulders toward the crossbar too soon during the take off, improper use of the inside arm, anticipating the roll over the bar by starting it too soon, and/or swinging the lead leg outside of the line of the body throwing it off balance.
4. Dislodging the bar on the upward part of the take off or on the downward part of the flight. If the take off spot is too close to the cross-bar, it will be dislodged on the upward flight; if it is

too far away from the bar, it will be dislodged on the downward flight. The take off spot must be firmly established, otherwise the effectiveness of the jump will be affected.

5. Diving over the bar. This is caused by several factors, such as taking off with the center of gravity moving too far ahead of the take-off foot. It is usually caused by shortening the last stride in the approach, driving the lead leg forward in a bent position and/or approaching the bar at an angle that is too narrow for the jumper.

6. Dislodging the bar with the take off leg. In the Western roll, this can be caused by failing to tuck the take off leg tight to the chest and dropping the head, arms, and shoulders toward the pit at the height of the jump. In the straddle roll it could be caused by improper timing of the take off leg at the height of the jump, such as failure to rotate the toe outward and upward, rotate the knee outward and upward, lift the leg and hip up and away from the bar, and/or turn the head toward the bar just after crossing it.

7. Sitting up over the bar. This is generally caused by holding the head too high as the body crosses the bar. Remember, a layout is encouraged by reaching toward the pit with the hands, shoulders, and head.

TEACHING BEGINNERS TO HIGH JUMP
Western Roll

The Western roll is generally taught before the straddle roll because it emphasizes a *jump* (kick and spring) then a layout over the bar. On the other hand, the straddle encourages the jumper to *roll* over the bar. Often beginners pick up a bad habit of starting the roll before reaching maximum height in the jump.

1. Determine the take off foot by running three strides then jumping in the air off of one foot. Repeat this exercise several times to see if the same foot is being used each time. Generally, right handed jumpers will use their left foot and vice versa.

2. Place the crossbar one foot above the pit. Using a forward approach, take three strides up to it, hop over the bar, and land on the same foot. Those who wish to take-off from the left foot form a line on the left side of the bar and those using the right foot, form a line on that side of the bar. Both groups will approach the bar at an angle of 45 degrees from their respective sides. A line or mark indicating the proper angle is designated by the teacher.

Figure 30. Common errors in high jumping. Turning the trunk toward the crossbar too soon; a lack of drive in the lead leg.

Figure 31. Common errors in high jumping. Anticipating trunk rotation too soon along with too little drive from the lead leg causes the hip and thigh to turn too soon. At this point the knee should be higher than the bar and the foot.

3. Using the 45 degree angles, the jumps are repeated. The teacher encourages a good extension of the take off leg as well as the trunk. Repeat this several times.
4. Jog up to the bar and swing the free leg up toward a diagonal corner of the landing pit; hop over the bar landing on the take off foot. The leg may be partially bent or extended. It would be wise to encourage a partially extended position.
5. Again, jog up to the bar, kick the free leg up, followed closely by a spring off of the other leg. Land on the take off leg. Repeat this exercise several times, emphasizing the kick then spring sequence.
6. Raise the bar to two feet. Attention is now focused on movement of the take off foot. Repeat number five but this time emphasize extending the take off leg as the push is made against the ground. It is then pulled as close as possible to the chest as the body passes over the bar. Land on the take off foot. The body maintains an upright position during the take off and landing.
7. Place a small object, such as a piece of foam rubber, in the pit about one foot from the bar. It is placed to the right or left of the center of the bar depending upon the take off foot (to the left for those using their left foot). Jump over the bar with a kick then spring. At the height of the jump, the jumper reaches into the pit with the inside hand to pick up the rubber. At the same time, she drops her head toward the same shoulder and lands on the take off foot. This initiates a layout across the bar and this movement helps to raise the hips over the bar.
8. Combine all of the preceding movements — kick, spring, tuck the take off leg, and reach into the pit with both hands. Land on both hands and take off foot. The elbows and wrists along with the knee and ankle should "give" upon the impact of landing.
9. Raise the bar to three feet and repeat number eight. Gradually raise the bar high enough to encourage a good spring and tuck of the take off leg.

Straddle Roll
1. Use the same take off leg and kick-spring sequence.
2. Draw a line on the grass near the high jump area. Place the take off foot parallel to the line. Swing the free leg up and over the line, spring on the supported leg and land on the foot of the free leg. Repeat several times.

TABLE 9

OUTSTANDING PERFORMANCES IN THE U.S.A. IN THE HIGH JUMP

YEAR	HEIGHT	NAME	AFFILIATION
1936	5'-2½"	Annette Rogers	Illinois Catholic Women's Club
1941	5'2-3/4"	Alice Coachman	Tuskegee Institute
1948	5'6-1/8"	Alice Coachman	Albany, Ga.
1955	5'-6½"	Mildred McDaniel	Tuskegee Institute
1956	5'9-3/8"	Mildred McDaniel	Tuskegee Institute
1959	5'10"	Taisa Chenchek	U.S.S.R.-National Team
1966	5'7"	Eleanor Montgomery	Tennessee State
	5'8"	Estelle Baskerville	Tennessee State

3. Repeat number two, this time at the height of the spring, drop the head and trunk toward the ground.
4. Return to the pit and repeat number three. This time use the hands to absorb the landing along with the lead leg.
5. If a sawdust pit is used, practice lifting the take off leg and hip up at the height of the jump. If a foam rubber pit is being used, practice rotating the foot and knee outward and upward at the height of the jump.

The Approach
1. ' After the jumping style has been established, the approach should be established.
2. Working with a partner, one girl stands an arm's length from the center of the bar, facing the direction of the approach. For an example, a left footed jumper places the fingers of the right hand on the cross-bar while she is facing the left approach way.
3. She runs five strides in the direction of the approach. The partner watching the run indicates where the foot lands on the fifth step. Starting at this spot, the jumper approaches the bar in five steps and jumps up in the air. The partner again checks on the take off spot and its relationship to the bar. This is repeated several times until the correct stride pattern has been established. It is important that the speed used to stride away from the bar be the same during the approach, otherwise the length of the stride will be affected.

COACHING AND TEACHING HINTS

1. Early season work should deal with general conditioning and form.
2. Begin jumping at a low height until the approach (speed and number of steps) and form are well established.
3. While working on form, place the bar a foot below the jumper's best height. Do not work at this height too long, the jumper will become lazy because maximum spring is not needed.
4. When working on errors at their best height, lower the bar two inches below this height and concentrate upon perfecting the mistakes.
5. It is not necessary to jump every day, three times per week may be sufficient. The other work days should consist of running such as sprinting, hurdling and a 15-20 minute Fartlek.

SUMMARY OF RULES GOVERNING THE HIGH JUMP

1. All measurements should be made with a steel tape and it should

be made perpendicularly from the ground to the lowest part of the upper side of the bar.

2.   A competitor may at her discretion, start jumping at the starting height or at any subsequent height.

3.   Three consecutive failures, regardless of the height or heights at which such failures occur, disqualify the participant from further jumping. After one failure at a particular height, the jumper may forego her second and third attempts at that height and still jump at a subsequent height.

4.   The bar should not be lowered for anyone reporting late. She must start at the height of the bar at the time of her arrival.

5.   The take off must be from one foot.

6.   Knocking the bar off the supports or touching the ground beyond the plane of the uprights with any part of the body (without clearing the bar) will count as a failure.

Chapter 10

BASIC MECHANICS
OF LONG JUMPING

The long jump involves four primary factors that are essential to good jumping: 1) speed in the approach; 2) height on the take off; 3) keeping the feet in the air as long as possible; and 4) landing with the body rotating over the feet.

THE APPROACH

The length of the approach varies with each jumper. Many of the better jumpers use an approach that is approximately 100 feet in distance. A controlled speed is needed; therefore, the jumper attains approximately 85-90 percent of her top speed within this distance.

TAKE OFF

The take off involves two important principles:

1. Attaining maximum vertical velocity. [1]

    Considerable horizontal speed is maintained during the approach, but the jumper does not accelerate into the take off. Instead, she "gathers" in the last three or four strides before reaching the take off board, thus permitting herself to gain a more powerful push off as the leg straightens. Due to the horizontal speed, the take off rotates the body slightly forward as well as upward.

    "In an effort to gain maximum vertical velocity on the take off, resistance to forward motion is minimized. A maximum vertical impulse is directed through the center of gravity. The lead leg, head, shoulders, and arms are first accelerated upward before an additional vertical impulse is involved through a vigorous straightening of the jumping leg." [1]

2. Rotation.

    The body tends to rotate forward in a sagittal plane as it pivots over the take off foot. Backward rotation is encouraged if the last stride is too long, thus destroying the horizontal speed. [1]

3. Flight.

    Once the body leaves the ground the path of the jumper's center of gravity has been determined. There is nothing one can do to change the flight path while in the air. There are certain movements, however, which can be made by the legs in the air to make the jump more effective. Movements such as the hitch-kick and hang, keep the feet into the air as long as possible, thus gaining added inches on the landing.

LANDING

Ideally, the best landing position is one that continues the flight path of the center of gravity as far as possible. At the same time it provides the greatest possible horizontal distance between the heels and center of gravity without causing the jumper to fall backward when landing. (1)

BIBLIOGRAPHY

1.   Dyson, Geoffrey, *The Mechanics of Athletics.* London: University of London Press LTD, 1963, pages 139-140.

Chapter 11

TECHNIQUES OF LONG JUMPING

Compared to some of the skills found in the track and field program, the long jump is relatively simple.

Techniques of long jumping are divided into four parts: 1) approach, 2) take off, 3) flight position, and 4) landing. Regardless of the style used by the jumper in the air, the approach, take off, and landing are relatively similar.

The Approach

A jumper reaches 85-90 percent of her top speed in the approach. Maximum acceleration is not obtained because she would have trouble converting the horizontal speed into an upward lift.

The distance of the average approach for girls varies between 90 and 120 feet, depending upon the rate of acceleration by the jumper. Some girls have tremendous acceleration power; therefore, they will not need an approach that is as long as those who accelerate slower. The length of the approach is determined by the distance within which a girl can approach top speed and still control the various body movements during take off. The number of steps used in the approach depends upon the length of one's stride. Usually, 19-21 strides are used by the more experienced runners.

The jumper accelerates with smooth and even strides in the approach until sufficient speed has been reached. Going into the last four strides, she relaxes and "gathers" for the jump.

The Take Off

The take off is a continuous movement of the approach. As the jumper "gathers" herself in the last three or four strides, she relaxes and prepares herself for the jump. Without sacrificing forward momentum, maximum height is desired in the take off.

On the last step, the knee flexes slightly as the body settles, thus permitting the jumper to gain a much more powerful push-off as the leg is straightened. The trunk is in a relatively upright position to enable the free leg to reach upward and forward on take off. Instead of obviously shortening the last stride, most jumpers start making this adjustment during the "gathering" phase of the approach;

therefore, the last stride may be only four to six inches shorter than the normal strides instead of 10 to 14 inches.

When the foot touches the take off board, the leg flexes slightly as the body rotates forward over the heel and pushes off with a strong action from the ball of the foot. The take off leg extends vigorously as it begins to lift the body forward and upward. The knee of the opposite leg drives upward in a flexed position to aid in gaining height. The head, chest, and shoulders are also carried high to assist with the vertical lift while the arms, generally moving alternately with the legs or circling together, balance the body.

Flight Position in the Air

The path of the center of gravity of the jumper has been determined once the body leaves the ground; therefore, one of the first movements off the board is getting sufficient height. Thsi is accomp-

Figure 32. The hitch kick — sequence of action

lished by running off the board, keeping the head and chest up and arching the back. The next problem is to keep the feet in the air as long as possible. There are several techniques or jumping styles employed by the jumper to delay the landing by keeping the feet elevated as long as possible for a more effective jump. These styles are currently being used by jumpers to solve the problem. These styles are: 1) the "sail", 2) the "hitch-kick", and 3) the "hang."

1. The *sail* is the easiest style to learn. Once the body leaves the ground, the free leg drives up and reaches forward. The take off leg pulls forward with great force. Both legs are carried in a partially bent position while the body is in the air. In an effort to keep the feet up as long as possible, the jumper tries to keep the heels on a line even with the hips, well ahead of the trunk.

    The trunk is carried in an upright position with a minimum amount of forward rotation. At the same time the head, chest, and arms are carried high.

    As long as a good trunk position is maintained, this style may be used to stress height in the jump and elevation of the feet before landing.

2. The *hitch-kick* is used by most of the better jumpers. This style emphasizes completion of one step in the air. (See Figure 32)

    The lead or free leg drives upward and forward as the take off leg trails behind. The forward leg straightens out as it swings back in a circular movement. At the same time, the take off leg is brought forward and upward in a flexed position, but it straightens out when it reaches the front. The lead leg continuing its circulatory pattern, returns to a forward position with the take off leg. Both legs are held relatively high in preparation for landing.

    Usually the arms move alternately with the legs during the jump or they circle together in a backward direction. The back is partially arched as the head and chest are carried relatively high.

3. The *hang* is the most difficult style for girls to learn because of the need for tremendous strength in the abdominal muscles and hip flexors.

    After the take off, the lead leg drops down to join the take off leg which is flexed at the knee. Both legs seem to trail the body momentarily. For a brief instance the body appears to be hanging in mid-air. The arms moving together circle in a backward direction. After the high point of the jump has been reached, the legs swing forward along with the arms. (See Figure 33)

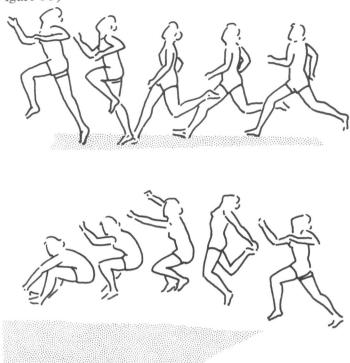

Figure 33. The hang — sequence of action

Landing (See Figure 32)

The landing is made with the legs extended forward as far as possible without causing the jumper to fall back in the pit. The head and trunk are pulled forward and downward in an effort to keep the hips from dropping into the pit. At the same time the arms are brought forward if they are carried high, or forward and backward if they are carried low.

LEARNING THE SKILLS OF LONG JUMPING

In order to learn the fundamentals of the long jump, beginners need to develop sufficient height and to learn to keep their feet raised as long as possible. Good extension of the take off leg and trunk should be encouraged with each style.

Each of the previously mentioned techniques will be briefly discussed. Before attempting to learn either style, the pit should be well dug to insure a soft landing.

The Sail

In addition to being relatively easy to learn, the sail is good for helping beginners gain height on the take off and to keep the feet raised as long as possible.

1. Determine the take off foot by using a short approach (five or seven strides). Take off on one foot, swing the free leg forward and upward, then land on both feet. Repeat several times to see if the same foot is being used.

2. With a short approach, take off by pushing against the ground and extending the take off leg. Swing the other leg forward and upward. At the same time keep the head and chest relatively high. Land on both feet.

3. Repeat the above take off movement, reach forward with both feet and land in the pit, in a seated position with the legs extended in front of the body. Try to lift the heels to the height of the hips while the body is in the air. The arms are extended forward for balance.

4. Repeat no. three and land on feet with the trunk and arms pulled forward.

The Hitch-Kick

Beginners have difficulty with this style because they do not have sufficient spring to keep them in the air long enough to move the legs. For this reason an aid such as a beat board or spring board may be used to help them gain additional spring.

1. Using a beat board, run up five strides, take off on the proper foot and land on both feet to get adjusted to the height attained with the aid.

2. Using five strides, run up smoothly to the board, take off on the proper foot and swing the other leg forward and upward. Land on the forward leg. Remember that the head and trunk are carried in an upright position while in the air.

3. Repeat movement 2; however, while in the air, the lead leg drops down and swings to the rear. At the same time, the take off leg swings to the front. Land on the take off leg with the other leg trailing the body.

4. Repeat the above movement 3. This time continue the action of the lead leg until it returns to the front. If the pit is extremely soft, the jumper should land in a seated position; however, if there is a question about its softness, the jumper should land on her feet with her trunk and arms forward.

The Hang

With the use of a beat board, beginners may also learn the hang.

TABLE 10

OUTSTANDING PERFORMANCES IN THE U.S.A. IN THE LONG JUMP

YEAR	DISTANCE	NAME	AFFILIATION
1936	18'	Mabel Smith	Tuskegee Institute
1939	19'4-5/8"	Stella Walsh	Polish-American A.C.
1948	18'4-5/8"	Emma Reed	Nashville
1956	19'9¼"	Margaret Matthews	Tennessee State Univ.
1957	19'5½"	Margaret Matthews	Tennessee State Univ.
1959	20'3"	Yera Krepkina	U.S.S.R.
1964	21'6"	Willye White	Chicago, Ill.

1. After the take off, the lead leg straightens out under the body. It swings to the rear flexed at the knee. This leg is joined by the take off leg which is also flexed at the knee. The trunk is slightly arched, in an extended position. At the high point of the body's flight path, the legs are brought forward and extended for the landing.
2. As the lower legs trail the body, the arms are circling in a backward direction. When the legs are pulled forward the trunk and arms are also brought forward in preparation for landing.

Approach

Once a basic style has been developed, the jumpers turn their attention to the approach.

1. Work in groups of two's letting one partner count for the other one.
2. One girl stands on the take off board with both feet. She sprints up the runway, fifteen strides, her partner counts the steps so that she will not have to slow down as she approaches the fifteenth step.
3. Starting at this spot, the jumper runs through the board. The first step of the approach is made on the take off foot. This is repeated several times to establish a stride pattern. If the foot is consistently behind or in front of the board, move the starting mark forward or backward a comparable distance.
4. As additional speed is developed, the starting post may be moved farther from the board. When the jumper runs nineteen or more strides, check marks should be used. The first mark indicates the starting spot, another one is placed opposite the seventh or ninth stride. If the proper foot hits the second mark, the same foot should hit the take off board without fouling. The run from the second mark should be smooth and unchanged.

HINTS ON LONG JUMPING

1. Develop an adequate approach with sufficient speed.
2. Keep the approach smooth, not a series of choppy steps.
3. Swing the arms vigorously at the take off and reach forward on landing.
4. Keep the chest and head up as the body leaves the board.
5. Regardless of the style, try to keep the feet in the air as long as possible.
6. Run off the board without stamping the foot; however the take off leg should extend vigorously as the body moves forward and upward.

Figure 34. Willye White, outstanding U.S.A. long jumper from Chicago. Notice the opposition arm action.

Figure 35. Mary Rand, outstanding English long jumper. Observe how both arms circle together.

7.   Always jump into a well dug pit that is filled with a soft substance.

PRACTICE SCHEDULE

1.   Jogging, loosening exercises, and speed work should be followed as in sprinting.
2.   Practice pop-ups (springing) into the air to emphasize a good lift and leg action.
3.   Practice horizontal bar work to develop the proper leg action.
4.   Engage in short runs with easy jumps emphasizing form.
5.   Practice running through the approach for a consistent step pattern.
6.   Work on sprinting speed.

ERROR IN JUMPING

Some of the major errors in jumping are listed below:
1.   Backward rotation of the trunk during take off. This is generally caused by reaching for the board with the last step.
2.   Too much forward rotation of the body during take off and in the air. In both instances, this is encouraged by using a stride that is too short, placing the body's center of gravity too far ahead of the take off foot.
3.   Dropping the feet too soon in landing. This is usually caused by too much forward rotation of the trunk.
4.   Falling back into the pit. This error may be caused by a backward rotation of the trunk.

GENERAL RULES GOVERNING THE LONG JUMP

1.   Each jumper is allowed three jumps. The seven best jumpers are allowed three additional jumps.
2.   Each jumper is credited with the *best* of all her jumps.
3.   The length of the run (approach) is unlimited.
4.   The take off board should be sunken flush with the ground. The outer edge of the board is called the scratch line. The ground in front of the scratch line is sprinkled with some soft sand to make it higher than the board.
5.   If a jumper touches the ground beyond the take off board, or an extension of its front line, the jump is not measured but it is counted as one of her required jumps.
6.   The measurement of the jumps are made at right angles from the scratch line or its extension, to the nearest break in the ground made by any part of the body of the jumper.

Chapter 12

BASIC PRINCIPLES OF THROWING

There are three different throwing patterns in the women's track and field program. Each one uses an implement that is different in size and weight. In spite of these differences there are several basic principles that are common to all of the patterns.

1. All throwing patterns are rotational movements. The discus rotates in a horizontal plane around the body, while the javelin and shot rotate in a vertical plane over the shoulder.

    The longer the radius of rotation, the faster the angular velocity for the same turning speed. This simply means that the thrower should try to keep the implement away from her body. For an example, the arm is extended sideways in the discus and backward in the javelin.

    There is also a strong hinge movement in the release speed of these implements. This speed is influenced by the movement principle which states "when a body moving in a straight line is suddenly checked at an extremity, a hinge movement results and angular momentum is developed." (2) The longer this "whip", the more speed it will impart to the implement.

2. To impart maximum speed to the implement, the body should be moving forward over the ground at the moment of release in all throws; that is, the feet are stationary on the ground, but the upper part of the body continues to move forward in the direction of the throw. (1) For an example, in the shot and discus the body continues toward the front part of the circle and in the javelin it continues toward the restraining arch.

    In order for the speed of the body to complement the speed of the throwing arm, the path of the implement when it is released should always be parallel to the path of the body during the acceleration period. (1) The javelin is a good example of this principle.

3. The speed of the implement depends upon the length of time force is exerted on it. This is why the shot putter leans over the rear edge of the seven foot circle before the glide. The discus thrower rotates in the eight foot circle, and the javelin thrower

extends the javelin well back in the last phase of the approach. (1)

4. The various forces of the body should exert a definite sequence of movement with proper timing in order to impart speed and power to the implement. The movement starts with pressure against the ground and each body lever in turn must be capable of moving faster in a given direction than the implement is moving in the same direction. The faster the lever can move, the greater will be its effective force. (2)

SEQUENTIAL MOVEMENT PATTERN FOR ALL THROWS

The basic movement pattern of the body in the throwing stance is similar for all throwing events; therefore, this pattern should be emphasized before concentrating on a specific implement. The following description is for a right-handed thrower.

1. The body is in a forward stride position with the feet about 24 inches apart and the weight shifted to the rear leg. The ultimate direction of the rear foot and knee will vary with the event. For simplicity, the body is at a right angle to the throwing direction with the rear foot and knee also pointing in this direction.

2. The rear foot pushes against the ground causing a lifting and forward rotation of the right hip as the leg extends the foot pivots to the front. This movement is followed very closely by a forward rotation of the trunk and an arching of the back. At the completion of this movement, the chest is high, the back is arched, and the trunk and stomach are facing toward the direction of the throw.

BIBLIOGRAPHY

1. Disley, John, *The Young Athletes Companion,* London: Souvenir Press, page 125.
2. Dyson, Geoffrey, *The Mechanics of Athletics.* London: University of London Press LTD, Second Edition, pages 165-168.

Chapter 13
TECHNIQUES OF
PUTTING THE SHOT

The put is a combination of speed and power imparted to the implement. Speed is gained by gliding across the circle while power is gained from the speed and strength of the muscles.

The put is made from a circle seven feet in diameter. A stop board is placed in the middle of the circumference in the front half of the circle. The shot is put in front of the shoulder with one hand. At no time should it be permitted to drop behind the line of the shoulder.

Although there are several techniques used to put the shot, the "O'Brian Technique" is the most popular style used by performers today. This style is considered effective because it permits the shot to travel through the greatest possible distance before it is released, thereby giving extra distance to the put.

SPECIFICATION OF IMPLEMENTS

The shot is a smooth, spherical implement made of solid iron, brass, or any metal not softer than brass. It should conform to the following specifications: 1) 4 kilograms (8 lbs. 13 oz.) and/or 2) 8 pounds. The official size for national and international competition is 4 kilos; high school girls and college women use the eight (8) pound shot in class and local meets. Junior high school girls use a six pound shot.

THE GRIP

The shot is held high on the fingers. To obtain this grip, rest it in the left hand, then place the right hand loosely on the top. For

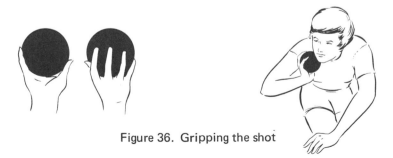

Figure 36. Gripping the shot

small hands, all four fingers are spread comfortably behind the implement for a better grip while the thumb offers lateral support. (See Figure 36) For a larger hand, the three finger grip is used. The thumb and fourth finger give lateral support to the shot while the other fingers are spread behind the implement. In either case, the shot is held by the fingers cushioned at the base of the fingers; it is not resting on the palm of the hand. It is important to have a well-balanced grip.

THE O'BRIAN STYLE

Initial Stance

The putter stands in a relatively upright position at the rear of the circle facing the outer edge. The shot is nestled under the jaw close to the neck and shoulder.

The elbow is under the shot; however, the arm is held midway between the shoulder and the side of the body. The line extending from the shot to the elbow along the forearm should be an extension of the line of flight of the implement as it leaves the hand. The other arm is extended above the shoulder. The eyes are focused on a spot about 10 feet behind the circle. It is important that the eyes focus on a spot and hold this focus because it helps the putter keep the head, shoulders, and hips facing this direction until the final rotation effort. (See Figure 31)

The Glide

The glide is initiated by a vigorous lift of the left leg. It moves up and back toward the front part of the circle. At the same time, the trunk drops forward until the back is extended almost horizontally. (See Figure 37 2-3) At this low point, the right leg flexes then extends, pushing the body across the circle. As soon as the right leg completes its thrusting action, the left leg drops to the ground near the toe board. (See Figure 37 4-5) The right leg remains partially bent.

At the completion of the glide, the body's weight is over the right leg, which is near the center of the circle. The right foot has made almost a 40° turn to the left in preparation for the pivot. The eyes are still focused on a spot approximately ten feet away and the left leg is near or touching the toe board. (See Figure 37 4)

The momentum initiated by the glide continues its forward movement even though the feet are not moving. Now the putter is in the throwing position; however, she is still facing the rear of the circle. (See Figure 37 5)

The Release

The large muscles continue to act upon the movement as the body begins to uncoil. The right leg thrusts against the ground lifting

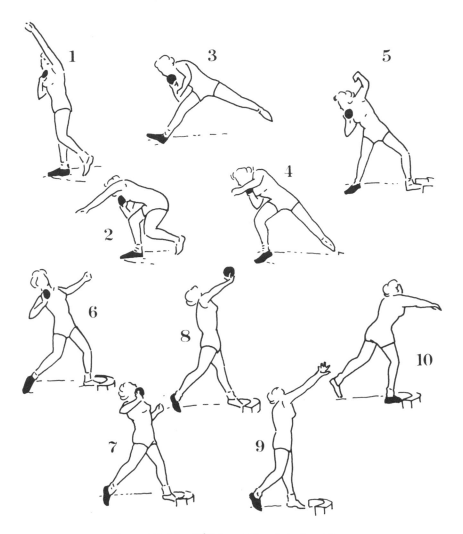

Figure 37. The O'Brian style of shot putting

and rotating the right hip toward the front. This is followed closely by rotating and lifting of the trunk and shoulders. (See Figure 37 5-7) The left arm, with a partially bent elbow, assists in the rotation of the trunk by its forceful pulling action. As the trunk completes its movement, the force initiated by the thrusting of the right leg moves through the arm. The elbow remains away from the body while the hand pushes up and away from the shoulder near a 40-45 degree angle. The fingers, being the last to leave the implement, impart a forward flicking action. (See Figure 37 8-9) It is important for the hand to remain behind the shot during its release.

As the shot leaves the hand, the putter extends her entire body. The force developed from the put pulls the body forward; therefore, a follow-through or reverse is used to maintain balance within the circle after the implement leaves the hand.

The Reverse

A second after the shot leaves the hand, the right foot leaves the ground shifting the weight from the forward or left foot to the right one. The feet are changing positions (See Figure 37 10) After balance has been maintained the putter leaves the circle by the rear half.

COMMON ERRORS IN PUTTING THE SHOT

1. Hopping across the circle instead of shifting across it.
    This is often caused by a lack of drive from the left leg just before the glide. It also interrupts the forward momentum of the body by creating an up and down motion.
2. Unbalanced body position after the shift.
    This is caused by weak thigh muscles of the supporting leg.
3. Inability to blend the glide, thrusting of the leg and rotation of the trunk together.
    This could be the result of the above errors, in addition to poor coordination of body movements.
4. Rotating the shoulders and trunk to the left during the glide.
    This is caused by anticipating the rotation too soon. Keep the eyes focused on a spot or an object until the glide has been completed.
5. Rotating the hips forward during the glide.
    This error is often associated with number four and the reason for the error is the same.
6. Dropping the shot behind or below the shoulder while rotating the trunk forward (throwing instead of putting it.)
    This is caused by allowing the hand to pull away from the neck as the trunk rotates forward. Keep the shot against the neck and the elbow behind it, especially during the rotation.

TEACHING THE SHOT PUT TO BEGINNERS

1. Hold the shot in the palm of the left hand and place the right hand on top of it. Grasp it so that it is resting on the base of the fingers, not in the palm of the hand.
2. Stand with the feet (parallel to each other) about eight inches apart, facing the direction of the put. Raise the left arm above the head and hold the shot in the right hand just under the

TABLE 11

OUTSTANDING PERFORMANCES IN THE U.S.A. IN THE SHOT PUT

YEAR	8 LB.	4 KILO	NAME	AFFILIATION
1936	41'8½"		Helen Stephens	Williams Wood College, Fulton, Mo.
1939	41'1-3/4"		Katherine Fellmeth	Chicago Park Hurricanes
1946	38'10-3/4"		Dorothy Dodson	Unat., Chicago
1948	40'3-7/8"		Frances Kaszubski	North Olmstead-Westlake A.C.
1951	41'3"		Amelia Bert	Little Rhody
1954	42'7"		Lois Festa	Red Diamond A.C.
1955		37'4-5/8"	Wanda Weizgrowicz	Polish Falcons
1956		46'9½"	Earlene Brown	Southern Pacific Association
1956	37'10½"		Dixie Griffin	San Fernando, Calif.
1960		54'9¼"	Earlene Brown	SPAAU – Los Angeles

chin by the neck. With the elbow midway between the shoulder and side of the body, push the shot up and away from the body.

3. Repeat the above movement by bending the knees, then extend the legs and push the shot away using about an angle of 45 degrees. During the early stages, it is important that the potential putter learn to use her legs and later her trunk when putting.

4. Again, using the above stance, bend the knees and rotate the body to the right as far as possible without moving the feet except for pivoting on the left foot. Uncoil the body and extend the legs, then push up and out with the arm. As the body uncoils, the trunk begins to arch and the head and chest are held high.

5. Stand in a forward stride position with the back facing the direction of the put. The feet are about 20 inches apart with the left foot closest to the throwing sector. Drop into the putting position by bending the knees and trunk. The body's weight is carried over the right foot. In order for the shot to travel through the greatest distance, the shoulders and head are carried near the edge of the base of support or just outside the edge of the circle, depending upon the strength of the individual. From this position, force is exerted through the foot, knee, and hip as the right leg extends and rotates the hip toward the front. This sequence is followed by an uncoiling of the trunk and shoulder while the right arm pushes up and out. The left arm pulls down and back in an automatic response.

The upward push with both legs is so strong that the movement carries the body slightly forward in its extended position.

6. After this phase has been accomplished, move into the glide. Draw a line seven feet long and stand near one end of the line facing a partner. Lean forward from the waist and hold the partner's hands for support and balance. Bend the knees slightly then swing the left leg back and up with vigorous action, allowing the force of the left leg along with a thrust of the right leg to shift the body approximately two to three feet down the line. The left leg reaches toward the other end of the seven foot line as soon as the right leg completes its shift. (See Figure 38)

Without the help of a partner, put the hand and arm in the putting position with an imaginary shot, glide across the circle trying to cover as much of the distance as possible. Remember to focus on an object or spot about ten feet away from the starting point.

7. Some girls will not have sufficient strength in the legs to master

the above shift across the circle. Therefore another style may be used by them for classroom purposes.

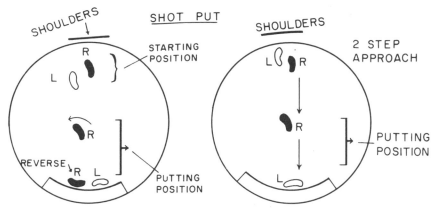

Figure 38. Glide pattern and two-step approach across circle

Stand with both feet near the edge of the seven foot line or circle. Lean forward from the waist and bend the knees, step back quickly toward the center of the line or circle with the *right* foot, take another step with *left* foot, this will put the putter in the putting stance. (See Figure 38) These two steps should be performed with as much speed and control as the putter can manage. Remember also, each step covers almost half of the over-all distance (seven feet).

8.   As soon as a reasonable amount of proficiency has been accomplished, combine the glide with thrusting action of the leg and uncoiling movement of the trunk. Try to make the movements continuous by blending them together.

9.   The reverse should not be taught until the other movements have been established and the putter finds herself having difficulty staying in the circle when the shot leaves the hand; otherwise, a beginner will find herself going into a reverse step with the shot still in the hand.

After the shot leaves the hand the right foot moves forward toward the toeboard and the left foot swings back. The weight and speed of the body is controlled by hopping several times on the right foot.

Each of the above steps should be practiced at first with an imaginary shot or a softball. A shot may be used as the proficiency of the individual improves.

Figure 39. Tamara Press, outstanding U.S.S.R. shot putter. Notice the extension of the body and the flicking action of the fingers (right hand).

TEACHING AND COACHING HINTS

1. Individual circles should be drawn on the track, grass, or surrounding area to allow large numbers to work at one time.
2. Emphasize keeping the shot against the neck under the jaw and pushing it up and out with a vigorous action.
3. Stress continuous action of the shot. The glide should blend with the put. It should not be a hop *then* put.
4. Stress the use of the entire body in the put, not just the arms and hand.

PRACTICE

1. Shot putters need to do a considerable amount of running and exercises that are designed to develop speed, strength, and coordination.
2. Each practice session should begin with easy puts from a standing position.
3. Some time is divided among the following parts of the put:
   a. Concentrate on form and the reduction of errors.
   b. Emphasize speed across the circle combined with a thrust of the legs.
   c. Concentrate on the angle of release and follow through with a reverse.

GENERAL RULES GOVERNING THE SHOT PUT

1. The shot should be put from the shoulder with one hand only. The hand should be in close proximity to the chin and it should not be dropped below this position during the put. Also, the shot should not move behind the line of the shoulder.
2. The putter should not leave the circle until the implement has touched the ground. She must leave from the rear half of the circle.
3. A foul is declared if a putter steps on or over the toeboard or the top of the circle while in the process of putting the shot.

Chapter 14

TECHNIQUES OF THROWING THE DISCUS

The discus is a very graceful event, yet throwing it correctly demands considerable speed, strength, and body coordination. The body of an official discus is made of wood or some suitable material with metal plates set flush into the sides. It weighs 2 pounds, 3½ ounces. The discus is thrown from a circle that has a diameter of 8 feet 2½ inches. Because of the limited space, the thrower takes a one and a half step or hop turn across the circle in order to gain momentum to impart to the implement.

The Grip

The discus is held in the hand with the fingers spread comfortably apart. The thumb is relaxed on the top of the discus. (See Figure 40) It forms an extension of the forearm. Only the fleshy part of the first joints of the fingers overlap the edge. Centrifugal force of the turn prevents it from slipping out of the hand.

Figure 40. Gripping the discus

THE ONE AND A HALF TURN

Initial Stance

The following description is for a right handed thrower.

The thrower stands near the rear edge of the circle with her back to the throwing sector. The feet are spread comfortably apart. Be-

118

ginners, however, have trouble starting in this position so they often begin one quarter of a turn to the left of this position using a one and a quarter turn.

Preliminary Swing

Several preliminary swings are taken to establish the rhythm of the movement. The right arm, fully extended, swings back to the right then forward across the body. The shoulder rotates with the arm. These swings are relatively relaxed, however, the body's weight shifts from one foot to the other during the swings. After two or three preliminary swings the thrower is ready to move into the turn.

The Turn

During the backswing of the last preliminary movement, the thrower begins to pivot. The right arm, held just below the shoulder, is extended away from the body and behind the trunk while the left arm is flexed across the chest.

Keeping the knees slightly flexed and the trunk upright, the thrower turns or coils to the right as far as possible, shifting the weight from the left to the right foot. The discus is carried as far as possible behind the shoulder in its coiled position so that it will trail the trunk as it uncoils. The head and eyes focus on distant objects in the direction of the spin.

At the end of the preliminary back swing, the thrower initiates a pivot to the left on the left foot, making about a 90 degree turn. As she continues to pivot on the left foot, the right leg drives across the left one toward the front, touching down near the center of the circle. (See Figure 41 & 42 1-11) The thrower is actually turning 360 degrees, while stepping toward the center of the circle. Trying not to interrupt the speed or the forward flow of the body, the thrower spins on the ball of the right foot. Continuing this movement, the left foot is then placed close to the forward edge of the circle just behind an imaginary line even with the right foot. (See Figure 41 and 42 12-13)

The Release

The thrower has completed a one and a half step turn. Throughout the entire turn, the discus has trailed the body.

As the left foot is planted near the front of the circle, the right foot begins to push against the ground causing an elevation and forward rotation of the right hip. This is followed very closely by an arching of the trunk and elevation of the chest as the trunk continues to rotate to the front. The left arm is used to help rotate the trunk toward the front of the circle.

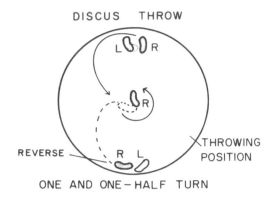

Figure 41. Discus throw — one and one-half turn

Figure 42. Discus throw — sequence of action

Following the action of the trunk, the right arm whips around the body with the palm facing the ground. The discus is released when the arm is almost level with the shoulder and parallel to the trunk. It is released at an angle of approximately 30-35 degrees to the ground. The index finger is the last to leave the discus. The pull of this finger causes it to spin clockwise as it floats in the air. (See Figure 42 16)

After the discus leaves the hand, a follow-through takes place. The right arm continues to move across the body and the body's weight is transferred to the right foot which then becomes the forward foot. (See Figure 42 18)

TEACHING BEGINNERS HOW TO THROW THE DISCUS
Holding the Discus
1. Hold the discus in the palm of the left hand, then place the right hand on top of it. Spread the fingers evenly apart, with the fleshy part of the first joints overlapping the rim. The thumb lies flat on the surface of the discus forming an extension of the forearm.
2. Let the arm swing back and forth around the body to get the feel of the discus. If the thrower has trouble keeping it in her hand, she should bend the wrist a little to let it rest on the forearm.

Releasing the Discus
1. "Bowl" the discus on the ground to a partner using the same motions as an underhand throwing pattern, that is, swing the arm backward then forward permitting the discus to roll off of the index finger last. On a good release, the discus will roll in a straight line toward the partner.
2. Using a horizontal swinging pattern around the body, release the discus at the side, off of the index finger. A palm-down position of the hand is maintained at all times.

Preliminary Swings
1. Stand in a forward stride position facing the direction of the throw.
2. Holding the discus in the palm of the left hand near the shoulder, place the right hand on top of it using the correct grip.
3. Swing the discus out and around the body to the right, let the shoulders and trunk turn in the direction of this movement.
4. At the height of the backswing, the discus is swung toward the front, returning to the left hand which is near the shoulder.
5. Throughout these swings, the knees are bent slightly and the

Figure 43. T. Press, U.S.S.R., end of preliminary backswing

Figure 44. Olga Connolly, U.S.A., releasing the discus

Figure 45. Olga Connolly, U.S.A., follow through of discus throw

body pivots on the left foot. Also, the body is relatively relaxed trying to make the entire movement as smooth and balanced as possible.

Standing Throw

1. Stand in a forward stride position with the feet about 24-30 inches apart. The right foot is turned out approximately 45 degrees and the left toe is on an imaginary line even with the heel of the right foot.
2. Shift the weight toward the right foot, bending the knee over it. The left leg forms a relatively straight line with the trunk. Rotate the trunk to the right until the shoulders are facing the opposite direction. Keep the right arm extended below the shoulder and behind the trunk with the palm turned down or slightly open. Care is taken to tuck the hips slightly under in order to keep them from sticking out too much. The left arm is about shoulder level in front of the chest.
3. Push against the ground with the right foot. This movement initials a chain reaction which begins with an extension of the same leg, followed by an elevation and rotation of the right hip, then the trunk rotates toward the front of the circle. The chest and head are carried high throughout this movement. The arm follows the trunk. The speed of the uncoiling action of the trunk pulls the right arm around the body *after* the trunk faces the forward part of the circle. The left leg extends and braces the body as the weight moves forward and upward. The discus is released just below the shoulder as the arms move into a position parallel to it. Remember, it should have a clockwise spin off of the index finger.

The Turn (One and a Quarter)

The turn, executed correctly, will add distance to the throw.
1. Draw a line eight feet, two and one-half inches long in the direction of the throw.
2. Stand near the rear part of the line at a right angle to the throwing direction.
3. Pivot on the left foot, turning to the left. The right leg drives across the left leg toward the center of the line. The body makes a 3/4 turn. In the final step the left foot is placed near front edge of the line. The right leg extends, driving the hip and trunk to the front. The reverse is the same as that used in the one and a half turn.

As the body turns, the thrower should allow her head to lead the movement, focusing the eyes on distant objects throughout the turn.

Each of the above steps should be practiced first without the discus, then with it.

COMMON FAULTS AND THEIR CORRECTION

1. Allowing the eyes to focus on the ground during the turn and the throw. Focus on distant objects that are eye level. The position of the eyes is vitally important to balance during the throw.
2. Allowing the discus to *lead* the trunk during the turn instead of following it. The basic principle of the turn is that momentum of the body must be established first, then transferred to the arm and hand. Allow the hand to rest on the lower back to establish the relationship of the arm to the trunk during the turn. Then extend the arm away from the body and behind the shoulder.
3. Failing to use the legs as a source of power in the throw. Drive the right leg to initiate trunk and hip rotation. Also use the left leg to check the rotation of the lower part of the body and to force the body up as the arm pulls through.
4. Allowing both feet off the ground during the throw. Considerable power is lost if the body is in the air during the release. Even though the body is extended during this movement, try to keep the feet in contact with the ground in order for them to apply as much force as possible while the discus is in the hand.
5. Releasing a discus that wobbles in flight. Usually this is caused by too much pressure of the thumb and/or permitting the second finger to leave the implement last instead of the index finger.
6. Releasing the discus off of the little finger instead of the index finger. Usually this is caused by failing to abduct the wrist during the release.
7. Failing to cross the circle in a relatively straight line. Often, beginners have trouble moving in the proper direction during the turn because their steps are too small. Practicing the turn on a directional line will help to give the thrower a better sense of direction.

RULES GOVERNING THE DISCUS

1. The discus is thrown from a circle which has a diameter of eight feet two and one-half inches.

2.   The thrower must remain in the circle until the implement touches the ground. Then she must leave from the rear half.
3.   The measurement of each throw is taken from the nearest mark made by the fall of the discus to the inside of the circumference of the circle along a line from the mark to the center of the circle.
4.   A valid throw must fall within a sector of 60 degrees that is marked on the ground.

TABLE 12
OUTSTANDING PERFORMANCES IN THE U.S.A. IN THE DISCUS THROW

YEAR	DISTANCE	NAME	AFFILIATION
1936	121'6½"	Helen Stephens	Williams Wood College, Fulton, Mo.
1938	126'¼"	Catherine Fellmeth	Dvorak Park, Chicago
1941	113'10-3/8"	Stella Walsh	Polish Olympic Women's A.C.
1948	124'3-3/4"	Frances Kaszubski	North Olmstead-Westlake A.C.
1953	123'2"	Janet Dicks	Harrisburg A.A.
1956	145'4½"	Earlene Brown	SPAAU - Los Angeles
1957	145'8"	Olga Connolly	Unat. Boston
1959	181'1½"	Nina Ponomareva	U.S.S.R.
1960	176'10½"	Earlene Brown	SPAAU - Los Angeles

Chapter 15

TECHNIQUES OF THROWING THE JAVELIN

The javelin is one of the most graceful throwing events; however, it is also the most dangerous one. For this reason, it is an event that is suitable only for girls of senior high school age and older. Even then extreme care must be taken when the javelin is being used.

A softball, baseball, or basketball throw is often substituted for the javelin in areas where it is prohibited. The movements required in throwing these balls for distance are very similar to that of the javelin, so there is little difficulty involved in changing to the javelin at a later date. With this in mind, the same approach and body movements should be taught to the young girls interested in throwing the various types of balls in place of the javelin.

The javelin is thrown from behind an arc of a circle drawn with a radius of 26 feet, three inches. Parallel lines, 13 feet, one and one-half inches apart extend from the extremities of the arc making the runway or approach. It is thrown into a sector of approximately 28 degrees.

The javelin consists of three parts: 1) a metal head, 2) a shaft, and 3) a cord grip. The shaft is constructed of wood or metal. Attached to the shaft is a metal head which forms a sharp point. The cord is located at the center of gravity of the implement. It weighs one pound, five and one-quarter ounces and it has an overall length varying from seven feet, two and five-eighths inches to seven feet six and one-half inches.

The Grip

The javelin lies diagonally across the palm with the tip of the thumb resting on the top of the binding. The index finger is curled lightly around the shaft, while the second finger is curled around the *top* of the binding. The other fingers are curled around the binding. (See Figure 46)

The Approach

Approximately 15-17 running strides are used in the approach. The speed of the run varies with the individual. Usually, it is a relaxed run with easy strides after a smooth acceleration. The javelin is thrown on the run. It is essential that the momentum of the body

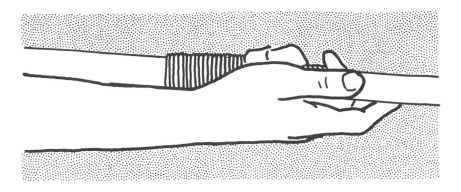

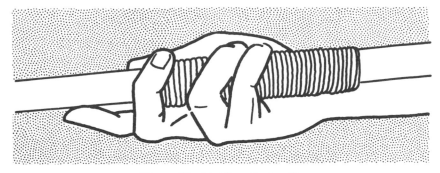

Figure 46. Holding the javelin

be maintained throughout the approach because the force of the
javelin depends upon a combination of body momentum and explosive power which is transferred to the javelin at the last moment.

The javelin is carried above the shoulder near the top of the head.
The point is forward while the implement is parallel to the line of
the run. The over-the-shoulder carry permits control of the javelin
during the approach and it minimizes the amount of rotation in the
arm as it extends back.

About 25 to 30 feet from the scratch line, the thrower begins
to rotate her body into position for the throw, while at the same
time, continuing the forward momentum. Thus, she is trying to
achieve top velocity of the javelin at the moment of release by continuing as smoothly as possible the body momentum and body force.

Cross-Step

The last five steps of the approach are important because they
put the body in position for the throw while continuing the forward
momentum.

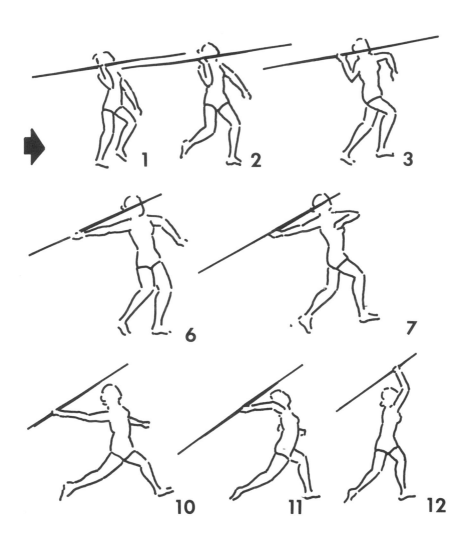

Figure 47. Javelin throw using two cross steps

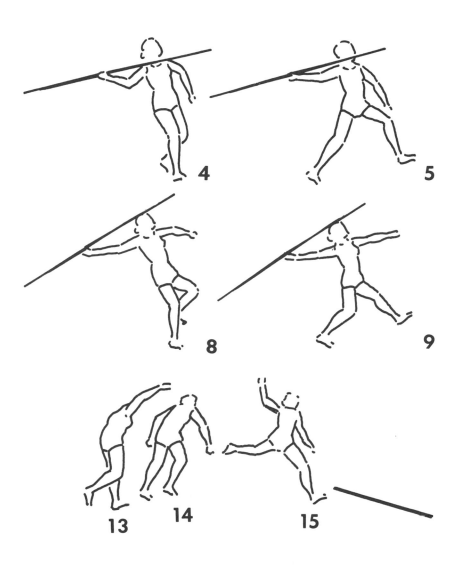

4

5

8

9

13

14

15

Up to this point the javelin has been carried over the shoulder. Now, starting on the left foot, each step lands with the toes pointing slightly to the right as the feet turn to the right with each step, the trunk rotates also in this direction. The first, second, and third steps are used to draw the arm back and carefully align the javelin over the shoulder so that the tip of it is parallel with the head of the thrower. The arm is relatively straight and is carried about shoulder level. The palm is carried in a palm-up position. During the third step, the trunk should complete its rotation to the right and the arm should be relatively extended.

On the fourth step, a "front cross-step" is executed by placing the right foot across the left to continue the forward momentum of the body while the hips and trunk turn sideways in order to extend the arm over the greatest possible distance. (See Figure 47 3 & 7) On the fifth step, the left leg quickly reaches forward in front of the body to act as a brake to stop the forward momentum of the legs. (See Figure 48) This also begins a hinge movement of the rest of the body. The body leans back, thus gaining more distance through which the javelin can move. (See Figure 47 9-10)

Throughout these steps, the right arm remains relaxed and straight while the left arm is carried slightly bent across the trunk for balance.

The Release

In a sequence of movements, the body's weight is over the right leg which is partially bent. (See Figure 48) The right leg extends then lifts and rotates the hips and trunk to the front. The back is arched. The trunk pulls the shoulder around then the elbow, heading this phase of the action, the elbow is bent and raised while the hand pulls forward and upward. The javelin is then pulled forward over the shoulder as the head inclines to the left to move out of the way of it. (See Figure 47 11) Since the fingers are the last to leave, they impart a rotation to it. The javelin is released at an angle of 38-45 degrees. A "Held" javelin is tapered to sail at an angle close to 38 degrees, whereas wooden javelins respond best to angles close to 45 degrees.

During the release, the body's weight shifts from the rear foot to the forward one as it moves forward.

Follow-Through

Both feet try to remain in contact with the ground until the javelin leaves the hand. The force of the body pulls it forward. The right foot swings forward in front of the left one while it swings back. The thrower allows several feet in front of the release point but behind the scratch line for the follow-through so that the momentum of the run and throw will not cause her to foul as she bounces forward. (See Figure 47 13-15)

Figure 48. Throwing stance of Polish javelin thrower

TEACHING THE JAVELIN THROW

1. Stick the javelin in the ground, kneel by it, and place the fingers around the cord as described earlier. Keep the palm of the hand behind the javelin and the forearm in a straight line down the shaft toward the point. Pull the javelin up and carry it over the shoulder. The javelin should rest diagonally across the palm of the hand.

2. Focus on a spot about 10 feet in front of the body. Point the javelin downward and spear it in the ground. It should stick in the ground. A follow-through should be emphasized with this movement.

3. Gradually lengthen the throwing distance from 10 feet to 20 yards. Check often to see that the fingers impart a clockwise rotation to the javelin as it sails in the air and that it moves in a

straight line ahead of the body. As the throwing distance increases, the point of the javelin tips up to a position to 30-40 degrees from the horizontal.

4.   Stand with the javelin above the shoulder facing the throwing sector. Step forward on the left foot and turn the trunk and hips to the right. At the same time, the right arm is extended back. Pull the hips, trunk, and right arm forward concentrating on the shoulder, elbow and hand coming into the movement above the shoulder in that order. (See Figure 49)

Figure 49. Throwing stance for a beginner

5.   Start again with the javelin above the shoulder facing the throwing sector. Step forward on the *right* foot, turning it at the same time to the right. The trunk and hips are also rotated to the right as the throwing arm extends back. Notice the forward cross-step of the right leg caused by the rotation of the trunk. Take a big step forward with the left foot. As this foot touches the ground repeat the latter part of number four.

6.   Take three steps starting with the left foot then repeat number five. Start extending the arm with the first step. Add a fourth and fifth step.

7.   Combine the five-step approach with the release of the javelin. Emphasize the "cross-step."

8.   Gradually combine the running approach with the completed throw.

COMMON ERRORS AND THEIR CORRECTION

1.   *Speed of the Run*

An approach that is too fast or too slow will detract from the performance. If it is too fast, the thrower will find it diffi-

TABLE 13

OUTSTANDING PERFORMANCES IN THE U.S.A. IN THE JAVELIN THROW

YEAR	DISTANCE	NAME	AFFILIATION
1936	125'¼"	Martha Worst	Palo Alto, Calif.
1939	130'9½"	Dorothy Dodson	Chicago Park Hurricanes
1948	140'4"	Dorothy Dodson	Mundelein, Ill.
1955	150'1¼"	Karen Anderson	Mercury A.C., Landsdowne, Pa.
1956	159'1"	Karen Anderson	Landsdowne, Pa.
1957	157'8"	Marjorie Larney	Queens Mercurettes
1959	181'8"	Berute Kaledene	U.S.S.R.
1966	188'11"	RaNae Bair	San Diego, Calif.

TABLE 14

OUTSTANDING PERFORMANCES IN THE U.S.A. IN THE BASEBALL THROW

YEAR	DISTANCE	NAME	AFFILIATION
1931	296'	Mildred Dedrikson	
1938	261'7"	Betsy Jochrum	Unat., Cincinnati, Ohio
1941	260'10-7/8"	Angela Mica	St. Louis A.C.
1947	252'8"	Marion Barone	Philadelphia Turners
1952	255'9"	Marion Brown	Deer Park, Tex.
1953	268'9"	Marion Brown	Gulf
1956	269'5½"	Pamela Kurrell	San Francisco
1957	271'10"	Mrs. Earlene Brown	SPAAU

cult transferring the momentum of the run into an explosive release. If it is too slow, there will be a definite lack of explosive power transferred to the javelin.

2. *Alignment and Trajectory of the Javelin*

The line of the javelin should be parallel to the line of the body. A loose grip and a partially turned palm will affect this line, causing the javelin to point toward the right or left. Also, in the cross-step approach, failure to turn the trunk toward the right as the arm is extended limits the amount of arm-reach and rotation of the palm.

Ideally, the javelin should be released close to 45 degrees to the horizontal. However, the metal Held-type javelin permits it to be released at a small angle (30-38 degrees) because of the improved aerodynamics giving it more glide at the end of the flight.

3. *Throw on the Run*

Often beginners will have difficulty throwing on the run. They will run, stop, and then throw. The purpose of the run is to impart more speed and power to the javelin; however, if the run is lost, power is also lost. Constant work on the approach will help to solve this problem.

PRACTICE SCHEDULE

1. Warm-up with jogging, wind sprinting, stretching and strengthening exercises.
2. Practice throws for form over a short distance.
3. Practice the last part of the approach, the last five steps.
4. Combine the approach and throw without using maximum effort in the release.

GENERAL RULES FOR THROWING THE JAVELIN

1. The javelin must be held by the grip with one hand. The little finger is nearest the point and the thrower's last contact with the javelin should be with the grip.
2. At no time after preparing to throw until the javelin has been discharged in the air, may the competitor turn completely around so that her back is toward the throwing area.
3. The javelin should be thrown over the shoulder or upper part of the throwing arm. It may not be slung or hurdled with an underhand motion.
4. No throw is valid unless the tip of the point of the javelin breaks the ground upon landing.

BIBLIOGRAPHY

1.   U.S.A. Official 1967 Track and Field Handbook. New York: The Amateur Athletic Union of the United States, pp. 148-9.

Chapter 16

ORGANIZING A TRACK AND FIELD PROGRAM AND MEET

ORGANIZING THE PROGRAM

Track and field programs for girls and women are organized on two levels within the United States — (1) schools (high schools and colleges) and (2) clubs. Both types of organizations give the United States its athletes for National and International competition.

The organizational structure of the program is very similar for the schools and clubs. Perhaps the only major difference between the two are the methods used to secure a budget, arranging transportation to meets, and arranging the use of local facilities for practice. Therefore, the discussion in this chapter will be limited to three main areas that are common to both groups.

1. *Stimulating an Interest in the Program*

There are many attractions in the school and community which are vying for the time and energy of our young people. In order to attract them to the track and field program they must see it as a challenge and an opportunity to develop within themselves individual skills that will give them an opportunity to meet their immediate and future individual needs.

There are numerous ways of stimulating an interest in this program. Listed below are only a few of them.

A. *Conduct workshops or clinics*

Invite an outstanding person to conduct a workshop for the students. The girls will show a great deal of interest and enthusiasm in the sport after hearing and participating in a workshop. They will be eager to put into practice some of the techniques and theories introduced at the workshop.

B. *Show track and field films*

Films are just like pictures — one film is worth more than 10,000 words. A colored film of the recent Olympics is generally an effective opening. This may be secured from The Olympic House, 57 Park Avenue, New York, New York. Loop films, such as those produced by the Athletic Institute, demonstrating individual events in regular and slow motion are equally effective. Another set of loops and a film will be completed very soon by the U.S. Women's Olympic Track and Field Committee. These films will illustrate efficient styles in the various events.

C.   *Promote interclass and intramural meets*
Annual interschool and intramural meets offer an opportunity for the inexperienced girls to participate against themselves. The meet should be well organized. Class and school records should be established.

The program should include all of the regular events covered in class. Several weeks before the meets, announce the dates, and help the teams to organize themselves. A copy of the rules and records should be made available at the beginning of the practices.

D.   *Use school publications*
The school newspaper is a good media. Submit or encourage the sports writers to feature some of the track and field activities. Also encourage them to include articles about your program.

E.   *Use the bulletin board*
The effectiveness of the bulletin board depends upon its location and the continued care given to it. An attractive display on the board that is kept up to date with fresh and new material is quite eye catching. It should be conveniently located so that the girls may view it as they pass by.

2.   *Organizing the Team*
A.   *Plan the organizational meeting*
Invite all interested candidates to join the group. Place the invitation on the bulletin boards, as well as in the school paper. Repeat the invitation several times over a two week period.

The first meeting of all interested participants should be a review of the scope of the program. It should include such items as the type of personal equipment needed; the importance of a good diet and adequate rest; the time designated for practice; the dates of possible meets; a review of the rules the girls are expected to follow; the importance of 100 percent effort at all times; and the importance of team effort.

During the meeting each girl should fill out an information card. It should include her name, address, phone number, age, height, weight, class, shoe size, shirt, and short size.

B. *Outline a challenging training schedule*

Develop a training schedule that will keep the group interested in the program. If it is too easy or too hard, many will become disinterested and drop out.

Let the girls experiment with several events before settling on a definite one. Often, it will take some of them a year or two to find their "best" event. Encourage them to participate in the events in which they show the most promise of success. This, however, is not always the event they would choose first.

C. *Secure basic equipment*

The school should furnish the basic equipment such as starting block, high jump standards and cross bar, hurdles, as well as the throwing implement.

3. *Effective Teaching and Coaching*

A. *Give individual attention*

Organize the practice so that each girl will receive some individual attention. This is very difficult to do with large groups; it will require the assistance of several of the team leaders (knowledgeable performers and managers). Basically, this is a good method because it not only helps the beginner, but the other participants are forced to analyze and understand their own events in order to explain them to others.

B. *Teach the fundamentals*

As the training schedule develops, the basic fundamentals should be stressed in all events in order to help the girls to perform the skills as efficiently as possible. Later, individual traits will blend with the fundamental skills and individual styles will unfold.

Establish individual goals with each girl as far as possible. The goals may be short range and long range. Try to aim for a standard at mid-season and another one for the end of the season.

C. *Plan a daily schedule*

Write out a daily schedule for each general area (sprinters, hurdlers, high jumpers, etc.). Make it available to the group and encourage them to develop the initiative and self-discipline to start working without immediate supervision. This is not a substitute for personal supervision, but it will permit the group to proceed with some phases of their training until the coach has an opportunity to rotate to each group.

D. *Consider individual differences*
Each girl will respond to coaching in a different way. Handle the girls in the best interest of the group. Special consideration is needed for the "problems" associated with those who are overconfident, easily psyched out, injury prone, and uncoachable.

ORGANIZING THE MEET

All track meets should be carefully planned. Good planning takes months to accomplish. The number of people involved in the meet depends upon the size of it. Small meets are generally organized by the teacher or coach, whereas the larger meets are organized by a local Games or Meet Committee.

The following responsibilities are initially assigned to the teacher, coaches, or Games Committee.

1.   Select the date and site of the meet.
2.   Select a list of events for the meet.
3.   Develop a time schedule for the events. Try to avoid scheduling together those events which will attract the same people, such as the 50 yard dash and 100 yard dash.
4.   Draw up a list of teams to be invited to the meet.
5.   Mail the entry forms along with an information sheet at least one month before the meet. The entry forms should include the schedule of events, the number of events each person is permitted to enter, rules governing the meet, time, and place of the meet, and a deadline for returning the entry form. The informational flyer should include data about housing (if necessary), eating, directions to the track, and dressing facilities.
6.   Select qualified people to serve as officials for the meet. The officials include a referee, clerk of course, starter, timers, scorer, finish judges, inspectors, head track judge, head field judge, judges for various jumping and throwing events, and announcer. In addition, someone should be appointed to serve as custodian of all equipment.
7.   Once the entries have been returned, preliminary heats should be drawn up by the meet director along with the order in which the jumpers and throwers are expected to compete.
8.   Competitor's numbers, awards, record cards, starting gun, stop watches, blank cartridges, starting blocks, measuring tapes, whistles, finish tape, and throwing implements should be assigned to one or two people for distribution at the appropriate times.
9.   Assign a person to take care of the pits and hurdles.

10. Make the necessary arrangement for marking the track and field.

Additional information about the conduct of meets, current rules, and the specific responsibilities of the officials may be found in the current A.A.U. official Track and Field Handbook (231 W. 58th St., N.Y.) and the current DGWS Track and Field guide (1201 Sixteenth St. N.W., Washington, D.C.).